DISCARDED

THE WABASH.

THE GRAVE YARD ON THE WABASH

THE WABASH:

OR

ADVENTURES

OF AN

ENGLISH GENTLEMAN'S FAMILY

IN THE

INTERIOR OF AMERICA.

> ——The forest glades,
> The spreading prairie, woo'd us on.
> Imagination, 'neath the shades
> Of timber'd wildernesses, ran;
> And lighted up the unknown land
> With hope and love and life renew'd:
> For Thou wast there; and, hand in hand,
> Bravely we met the forest rude.

BY

J. RICHARD BESTE.

IN TWO VOLUMES.
VOL. I.

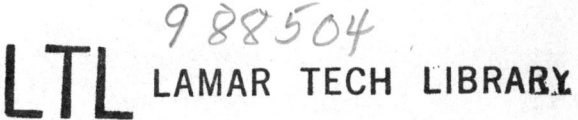

BOOKS FOR LIBRARIES PRESS
FREEPORT, NEW YORK

First Published 1855
Reprinted 1970

STANDARD BOOK NUMBER:
8369-5456-4

LIBRARY OF CONGRESS CATALOG CARD NUMBER:
75-121498

PRINTED IN THE UNITED STATES OF AMERICA

PREFACE.

The following pages contain an account of the adventures of a family, in the rank of English country gentry, during their travels into what Europeans consider the Backwoods or the Far West of North America. I am aware that the lapse of thirty or forty *months* since they took place, would make a description of the cities of the United States as much out of date as would the same number of *years* intervening after a visit to the towns of the Old World; but I did not linger in the long-settled States of America nor in their capitals.

Although the villages and the towns and the countries which I most visited, may be now more filled up and " fenced in", yet will my description of them and of their inhabitants apply to localities, similarly placed in regard to the onward march of civilisation across that mighty continent, so long as a forest or a prairie shall remain uncultivated between the Atlantic and the Pacific—so long as the American people shall be an amalgamation of individuals transplanted and, more or less firmly, rooted by citizenship in the rich soil which it is given to them to fill and to subdue.

Travelling, as we did, with a large family of children, we were, necessarily, brought into contact with much of which a single male traveller hears and sees nothing:—I had to make thoughtful provision for our slow progress in the interior, where he would have sped fearlessly onward in his stage-coach or steamer. This has enabled me to describe much that he never sees. His greater independence of motion may, indeed, have oftener thrown him into companionship with those individual oddities and entertaining scamps whom we are, sometimes, told to look upon as types of the whole American people; but the incidents of family travel have afforded interests more deep, and, probably, more genuine.

In these volumes, will be found many passages purporting to be extracted from the written records of my children. I would mention that these records were not compiled by them with any view to publication, nor, even, from any love of writing about themselves; but because, as a task and to exercise the composition and the handwriting of the younger of them, I desired each one to write, and to bring me every day, some account of their travels in America. When these descriptions appeared to me graphic or entertaining; when they told the sad scenes which I myself was incapacitated from witnessing; when, even, they only showed the impressions which a new country and new scenes produced upon new minds — I did not scruple to embody them: because I felt that I could so best fulfil the object I had in view, that I could so best familiarise the reader with America and the American people.

My endeavour has been to represent, in these pages, what we saw and felt: consequently, they must contain much that is personal; much that is light, frivolous, anecdotical; much, also, that is dark and sorrowing; for such was the course of our travels. Like the Swiss family Robinson Crusoes, we stand before the reader — mysteriously driven forth to wander and to live, for a few months, in a character as new to ourselves as our real position is unsuspected by those amongst whom we travel.

Whatever may have been this immediate cause of our journey—of which more anon—much of my serious inquiry did, I own, tend to the study of the United States as a scene for agricultural emigration. Those, therefore, who have more health and strength than money, and those who have more sons than means of advancing them in England, may gather from these pages the result of much investigation:—while those who care to know the social and religious state of the emigrant's future home, or only to see the Americans as they are amongst themselves in the far Western States—when they little think that he, whom they please to look down upon as a poor family emigrant, is a "chiel amang them taking notes"—these, also, will necessarily find here much matter suited to their lighter tastes.

 Grosvenor Street,
  30th April 1855.

CONTENTS OF VOL. I.

CHAPTER I.
BORDEAUX.

Residence in a convent.—The villa.—The climate.—The vineyards of Bordeaux.—The ex-minister, De Peyronnet, parboiled.—The archbishop and the curé.—Agen of the Fat Geese.—French doctors.—Vessels to America.—The plate chests.—The Belle Assize.—Emigration.—The Bosquet de Flore.—Departure.—Working consuls and gentlemen consuls 1

CHAPTER II.
"THE KATE HUNTER."

The lap-dog.—The parrot.—The dormouse.—The dream.—Search for a vessel.—The outward-bound.—Torbay.—Life on board.—Young "Go-a-head."—Captain Parsons.—Icebergs.—Mysterious causes of our mode of travel.—Our yacht.—Accidents.—The pilot.—Our invalid 33

CHAPTER III.

New York.

Quarantine.—The Custom-house officer.—Irish carmen and porters.—Our children on board.—Broadway.—American omnibuses.—The post-office.—The money-changer.—Speculation.—The cobler.—Hotels.—Gentle and simple.—A chambermaid.—Private rooms 64

CHAPTER IV.

The River and the Railroad.

A sharp man.—The Irish maid.—The river boat.—The Hudson.—West Point.—The railway *versus* the river.—Selling pets.—The New World aground.—Albany.—The sharp agency.—An Albany waiter.—The railway cars.—British delicacy.—First class trains.—The scenery.—Rome.—Oneida.—Cayuga Lake.—Geneva.—The burning spring.—Rochester 94

CHAPTER V.

Niagara Falls.

The "gals".—Buffalo.—The churches.—St. Patrick's church.—The lapdog.—The railway accident.—The runaway slave.—Roasting and shooting niggers.—Niagara Falls.—Goat or Iris Island.—The Horseshoe Fall.—Mr. Geo. W. Sims and the ferry.—Canadian and American manners.—The lost hat.—Canadian and American prosperity 120

CONTENTS. vii

PAGE

CHAPTER VI.

Lake Erie.

The mayor of Buffalo and the porters.—The night of of a nurse.—Lake Erie.—Cross questions and crooked answers.—Emigration.—Sandusky City.—Labels for railway luggage.—Through the forest.—Log-houses and frame-houses.—A worm fence.—Clearings.—Agriculture of Ohio.—Arrival at Cincinnati   146

CHAPTER VII.

Cincinnati.

The Burnet House Hotel.—The Queen City of the West.—Bill of fare in Ohio.—The cathedral.—The Catholics.—The author's politico-religious creed.—The calendar.—The ecclesiastical seminary.—The upper crust of Cincinnati.—Search for a location.—Porkopolis.—The ladies' saloon.—Honorary titles.—The banker.—Hours of business.—Engravings on paper money 175

CHAPTER VIII.

The Pledge.

Father Mathew.—Another pledge.—The cathedral.—Mrs. Trollope.—Incendiarism.—Jesuits.—Cardinals.—American Catholics.—Irish emigrants.—The Maine liquor law.—Forwards! . . . 211

CHAPTER IX.
THE OHIO.

Rivers of England and of America.—Kentucky or Ohio: freedom or slavery.—Plan for emancipation of slaves.—La Belle Rivière.—Vineyards.—Cholera.—Maddison.—The Mammoth Cave.—Aspect of Indiana 228

CHAPTER X.
INDIANAPOLIS.

Hotel at Indianapolis.—Punkahs.—Manners of Americans.—A gone 'coon.—Difficulty of going further.—An isolated priest.—Colonel and Mrs. Drake.—Plan of American cities.—A morning visit.—A spirit shop.—The Capitol.—Walks.—Buying horses.—Buying a wagon.—A carpenter.—American English.—Buying a location.—The *Indiana Sentinel.*—American newspapers.—Fashionable shops . . 225

CHAPTER XI.
THE WAGON.

Our new equipage.—Its triumphs and pleasures.—Highway robbers.—Baiting.—The Cholera House.—Long's House.—An American woman.—Mount Meridian.—The National Road.—Mr. Townsend.—Evening fancies.—Records of children.—Dr. Ushaw's.—A land-jobber.—Van Buren.—Premonitory symptoms 292

THE WABASH.

CHAPTER THE FIRST.

BORDEAUX.

Residence in a convent—The villa—The climate—The vineyards of Bordeaux—The ex-minister, de Peyronnet, parboiled—The archbishop and the curé—Agen of the fat geese—French doctors—Vessels to America—The plate chests—The Belle Assize—Emigration—The bosquet de Flore—Departure—Working consuls and gentlemen consuls.

BORDEAUX is a magnificent city. Its open squares, its " allées", its " courses" bordered by trees, and its public buildings, make parts of it more imposing than the best quarters of any other town in Europe—excepting, always, Paris. The private houses of its merchants and the magnificent colonnade of its theatre give evidence of the wealth of its inhabitants: and its countless shops of " charcutiers", piled with every delicacy, from Strasbourg and Perigeux pies to the native wines of the district, make the mouth of the stranger water, while he accuses the inhospitality of the préfet (M.

Neveu) which debars him from being introduced there where his excited appetite might be gratified, and the memory of the préfecture embalmed with that of trouffles and of fat geese from Agen.

Unlike the holders of most préfectures in France, M. Neveu treats English visitors to the town with marked neglect.

But strangers visit not Bordeaux as a place of residence. Instinct seems to have guided our travellers in the selection of quarters recommended by climate, by scenery, by cheapness of the necessaries and comforts of life, or by the hospitality of the natives; and none of these attract to Bordeaux. In vain, therefore, did we seek through every quarter of the town for a furnished apartment that we might lease for a time; a single room, or even two or three " chambres garnies", were to be had; but a house, or even a large furnished apartment, was no more to be met with than bashfulness in a Gascon.

At length, we turned us to the neighbourhood of the city. Our old banker, M. Guestier, told us that he had a château to let in what was considered the paradise of Bordeaux. We saw it; agreed to his terms; and were about to pay him a year's rent in advance, when he said, " I ought to tell you that I wish to sell the property, and must reserve the right of doing so."

" Be it so," I replied; " in that case, you must return an amount of the rent proportioned to the term which we shall have surrendered."

" Pardonnez-moi," he answered. " If I sell during the first three months of your occupancy, I will do so; but if after that time, I do not return anything."

I made my bow, and took an affectionate leave of M. Guestier.

Fruitless, however, were all our inquiries for a residence; till a good priest informed us that the nuns of Talence, near the banker's château, would let us the main building of their convent, reserving only a wing for themselves. We inspected and engaged it for a month.

" And why," asked the curé, when, at the end of the month, we removed to another house, "why have you quitted these good nuns?"

"I was fearful of growing into a nun myself, M. le Curé. I met nuns at every corner. Instead of having that wing of the house to ourselves, as covenanted, we found that the garret above us was the dormitory of the holy sisters; and there was, consequently, a continual rush of *religieuses* from the bottom to the topmost story. Was I going to the cupboard in the anteroom for a bottle of choice wine, a nun was sure to pop out of her neighbouring laundry upon me; on the staircase, I met a couple of nuns, with a plate of milk, coaxing a cat to follow them up to their dormitory; and once, in the dusk of the evening, as I was hurrying down to tea, I came full tilt against a veiled lady in black who was rushing towards the stairs, and to whom, mistaking her for my daughter, I opened wide my arms."

The Curé laughed amazingly.

"But I hope you parted from them on good terms?" he asked.

"On the best in the world," I replied. "Many little acts of politeness had passed between us and the reverend mother. Once upon a time, for example, our footman had, with much ceremony, introduced to our sitting room two of the nuns, bearing between them, like a royal crown upon a cushion, a small glass vase, about the size of a coffee cup, which they presented to us with much solemnity, and with the compliments of the reverend mother, who prayed that we would accept a 'pot de confitures' of their own making. Of course, we received it with all decorum, and eat the preserve with a kind of pious gastronomic delectation. But, however, in the bill that two of the sisterhood presented when we left the apartment, I was puzzled to read the following charge.

"'For a pot de confiture . . 0fr. 5c.'

"'Five centimes, one halfpenny for a pot of preserve!' I exclaimed: 'but, Mesdames, did we not enjoy that confiture as a token of your beneficence?'

"'But the pot, Monsieur,' answered the aide-de-camp, casting down her eyes and folding her hands in the sleeves of her ample dress; 'the charge of five centimes is for the glass pot that contained the confitures.'

"'A thousand pardons! forgive my stupidity!' I replied; and I bethought me of the story of the king of France and the dish of partridges."

"What is the story?" asked the curé.

"A king of France," I answered, "having much relished some stewed partridges, said to one of his people in attendance, 'Give that dish to Pierron, the fool.' Joyfully did the fool stretch to receive it, and, examining the gold dish with glee, exclaimed, 'What a beautiful platter! It is all gold! Thanks, Monseigneur, for your royal gift! But the stewed partridges—may I have the stewed partridges also?'"

"The anecdote is apposite," said the curé laughing; "though it is to be hoped that the circumstances are reversed in this instance, and that the preserve was worth more than the pot."

A majestic old lady, in truth, was the Reverend Mother. Barely five feet high, she must have been nearly as much in diameter; and she engulfed immense quantities of snuff as she told us how heaven had favoured her since she had run away from the house of her father, who objected to her taking the veil (this I thought a questionable piece of morality); and how, from the slim girl she was then, she had grown and grown while residing in Gascony and drinking Bordeaux wine. She expressed admiration of our large family; said that such were always blessed of heaven; and was most anxious to induce some of our daughters to remain with her.

" But, Madame!" I exclaimed, " if heaven approves large families, surely you would not counteract its possible designs by putting my daughters out of the way of fulfilling them—

" What's killing offspring, whether few or many,
To cutting off one's chance of having any ?"

" You think me silenced by your argument!" she cried triumphantly. " Know that I have many more children than you. This order of *religieuses*, it is I who founded it; and it already numbers more than four hundred and fifty members in France."

This was true: and the institution itself appeared to be an useful one. Although the Reverend Mother boasted herself to be of a gentleman's family, most of the sisters appeared to have been taken from the lower orders. In peace and piety, they devoted themselves to the instruction of poor children, while they cultivated little farms around the several houses they had established in many neighbourhoods of poverty and ignorance. Thus the vineyard around the convent was dug and cultivated by the sisters; the cows were watched and tended by them as they industriously knitted or turned the spindle; and the acacia poles (cut down to serve as props to support the vines) were peeled by them of their rind for no other reason that they were aware of, they told me, than that the Reverend Mother had ordered them to do so. I learned, however, from their labourer that, when thus peeled, they lasted much longer in the ground.

I am afraid that we all rejoiced to leave the convent; and to take possession of an entire villa in what was considered a beautiful garden in this same commune of Talence. The proprietor had been secretary to the Horticultural Society of Bordeaux; and the garden showed ample evidence to his love of flowers. It had greenhouses stocked with plants and with orange-trees in pots, that were carried out into the open air in summer. Straight rows of beech trees diverged from the front of the house, and these, being intersected by high hedges clipped and trimmed, gave us walks sheltered and shaded as much as the winter sun or the winds of that mild climate made requisite.

The climate of Bordeaux seems, in truth, to be a very mild one. Of winter, we had none. No high mountains are near to chill the air with their snowy mantles or intercept the salt breezes of the Bay of Biscay. The whole country about us was a dead flat:—beautiful to the eyes of the landowners, because it produced some of the best wines of the province; but the scenery of which was uninteresting to any but an agriculturalist—or a musician. I say a musician, because such an one only could enjoy the hoarse concert which made the whole air vocal from sunset till dark. The

Talence nightingales, as I somewhat annoyed the natives by calling them, then opened their mouths; and the croaking that arose from pools and ditches, invisible by day, was so widespread, that it really sounded like muffled drums or the tramp of distant cavalry.

The cultivation of the vineyards is a most laborious and scientific work. The vines are not swung from tree to tree as in some parts of Italy; nor are they left to trail on the earth, like weak gooseberry bushes, as in Provence: they are planted in rows and tied to poles, such as we had seen the good nuns peel " because reverend mother ordered them to do so". The earth between the rows is carefully dug with pronged forks two or three times during the summer, and mould is drawn round the roots: at the first digging, young plants are set in to replace those that have died, and manure is carefully laid at the foot of each. Twice are they pruned: and in such a manner as not to anticipate that of future years while preparing for the crop of the ensuing summer. The facility of doing this, in fact, prevents prudent proprietors of vineyards from letting their farms: the tenant might too easily secure the harvest of years, and exhaust the plants while pruning them apparently for his own crop. But as the labour, when fairly done, is quite one of routine, a foreman only is required to the most extensive vineyards. Each proprietor farming his own land knows how many diggings it ought to have, and what ought to be the charge for each: and each one knows how many barrels of wine each acre, or measure of land as they call it, and it is about the same, ought to produce. The value of the produce of a good acre of vineyard was about £30.

But complaints were then as loud amongst the wine growers as they are now. Bread was then so dear, that M. de Peyronnet complained to me that the people could not afford to buy the inferior coarse wines, such as the people only drink and such alone as his lands produced. He was a pleasant man, this Comte de Peyronnet, ex-minister of Charles X, who is said alike to have instigated and to have disapproved the ordonnances that caused his sovereign to be expelled from France. I met him, and was first introduced to him at a dinner party at the palace of the Archbishop of Bordeaux, now Cardinal Donnet. On entering I observed a very gentlemanly, good-looking man of between sixty and seventy, who, clad in tights and pumps, was affectionately nursing his left leg on his right knee: people were asking him about his lameness, and, when I was introduced to him, he explained to me, as to a stranger, how it had chanced.

"I had told my servant," he said, "to put in my bedroom a footbath full of warm water, as I wished to soak my feet: what did the fellow do but set it full of boiling water! I suspected nothing of this, and pulled off my stocking and plunged my foot in. The water was boiling, but, ma foi, I was not the man to retreat, 'je ne voulais pas broncher,' and so, as it was in, I e'en left it there. When I took it out, all the skin came off in the towel."

"Just the kind of obstinacy which cost his sovereign the throne of France," I thought.

"What a fool!" exclaimed a sensible Englishman, to whom I repeated the anecdote.

I never tasted such a variety of wines, nor

heard so much talk on their several merits, as at this dinner party at the Archbishop's. This was naturally the case. Amongst twenty-four people whose revenues were dependant upon wine, what subject could be so interesting? They tasted as farmers and connoisseurs: no one committed the slightest excess in quantity.

The Archbishop of Bordeaux, since made a Cardinal, had been brought to my house by the Curé of our parish, one day when he administered Confirmation in the church of Talence. Several members of my family had received the Sacrament from his hands, and so rare are English residents in that neighbourhood, that he could not but feel interested in us. I know not whether he was gratified or not by the extra homage we paid him by bending the knee and asking for his blessing when we were presented to him; but I found that modern France denies such honour to its Bishops. It is a question of etiquette. They had been preaching a mission, as it is called, at Talence; that is to say, for some weeks the Curé had been instructing his flock with extra care, and preparing them for the Confirmation; and, for the last fortnight, he had called in a priest from a distance to help him. The church had been crowded; for this was a new man, and was rather celebrated as a preacher. He not only discoursed well on his subject, but he tore it into tatters, and exhausted it and himself with his own vehemence: so different was his style from the sensible, argumentative, familiar, and sometimes impassioned though quiet eloquence of our own Curé, that all run after him, as a matter of course. M. le Curé was one of the cleverest and most exemplary of the many good parish priests I have ever met with. He was learned without pedantry; cheerful without levity; friendly with his flock, without familiarity. He was very fond of music, and selected a goodly number of boys and girls whom he assiduously taught to sing, while he accompanied them himself on a seraphine. He introduced a great deal of singing of *Cantiques* in French into the service, and he thus not only drew people to his church by giving them the pleasure of hearing their own sweet voices uplifted in verses which they understood, but he made the very *Cantiques* themselves popular throughout the district, to the exclusion of the profane ballads which they supplanted. I own I have been greatly surprised to hear noisy parties of men at the country wine shops, all joining in chorus and singing our Curé's *Cantiques* over their cups. Nay, the Archbishop himself, when he took us to see his country seat near Bordeaux, which he was very anxious we should rent, constantly forgot himself and began humming the Talence *Cantiques* as he wandered from tree to tree, noting the blossoms and the chances of a crop of fruit from his orchard.

They were contented men, the Curé and the Archbishop: the latter would have suffered from the failure of his little crops but that the Government paid him 6,000 francs (or £240 a-year) as an archiepiscopal revenue; and the Curé must have starved outright, but that the Government allowed him, in his quality of Curé, 800 francs (or £32) a-year. On these incomes, they were contented and merry. The Curé was rebuilding his pretty little church, and the Archbishop kept up all the state proper to his high rank.

That church at Talence was a favourite place of pilgrimage for the good people of Bordeaux, who made constant pleasure parties to it; and after hearing mass and fulfilling their vows, had merry breakfasts in the little garden and arbours around it. The Curé insisted that this was harmless and innocent recreation; and not the less so that religious devotions had preceded it; nor would he admit that the religious devotion was profaned by the friendly breakfast that was to follow. Of the miracles thought to be wrought by prayer in the sanctuary, he left each one to judge for himself. As the popular sentiment moved each one to more fervent prayer in the church of Notre Dame de Talence than elsewhere, their prayers, he said, were more likely to be granted; and hence virtue came to be attributed to the church itself. The Curé did express a wish that the people would not tie garlands of flowers and bits of tawdry finery round a mutilated colossal statue of an angel, which they took to be a Madonna, and which, having been removed from the old church when it was rebuilt, had been laid neglected against a tree in his garden. But the intention was devotional; and how could he risk offending the devotees of his parish by charging them with indecorum and apparent idolatry, of which they had never dreamed?

This fear of giving offence must always, more or less, act upon ministers who are dependent upon their flocks. On the day when the Archbishop had given confirmation in the church, the Curé had sent to borrow our fish-kettle, as the prelate was to dine with him, and a lady of Talence had presented him with a magnificent turbot. The kettle was lent, and we went to church: there we took our position in an open space near the altar; and when the good priest requested us to move elsewhere, I resolutely refused to do so, as I could not understand that the space was really wanted for the ceremonial. He urged me much, and said afterwards, " I knew I should get such a scolding for allowing you to stay there from Madame la Dévôte, for I had just turned herself from the place; and it was she who had given me the turbot!"

In the United States of America, all ministers of religion are dependent upon the support of their followers, and I was about to see how the principle would work there against a lady who gave a turbot!

One winter's morning about five o'clock, consequently in the dark, we made our way on board a little steamer that lay near one of the piers of Bordeaux; and when the sun rose, found ourselves going up a broad stream between flat and sedgy banks, above which nothing was to be seen on either side. There was a fair number of country people on the deck, which was encumbered with empty hen-coops, returning to the farmhouses which supplied Bordeaux with poultry and the famous fat geese of Agen. On—on went the steamer for about one hundred miles, and little could we see on either side beyond the reeds or the willows that covered the fenny banks. Occasionally, as near La Reolle or Marmande, a small bluff rose above the water; but there was no scenery that could be called the least pretty until we came to the dingy old town of Agen, with its narrow streets bounded by low-browed arcades, on which the old houses toppled over, as they seemed to have done for the last thousand years. Why, then, do I record this two days' trip up the great Garonne? I do so, because the mind, now looking back to a country where the government has created no public works, but where popular energy has covered the wilderness with animation, marvels to think of the many splendid bridges, erected by the state, that spanned this river from either side, while its waters, running through populous districts and into one of the busiest commercial sea-ports of France, were unthought of as a means of traffic, and bore upon their ample breast only our own miserable steamer and its fellow of the alternate days, and a few small barges that seemed to ply from village to village—heedless of the wide world which the ocean opened to them a few leagues lower down! So impossible is it for a government to supply the lack of individual and national energy! so impossible is it for national and individual energy to lie dormant, although unassisted by government!

And now, the time was at hand when we were to quit Talence, and seek those stirring wildernesses. One of my daughters had been seriously unwell. Dr. Chaumet, an eminent physician of Bordeaux, had attended her; and, with blisters and leeches, had checked what he believed to be a dangerous disease of the lungs. On the 7th of April, she was much better, and he told me he had hopes of restoring her health: "This month", said he, " I will give cod's liver oil: in May, she shall change it for eau de goudron: in June, she shall live upon ass's milk: in July, we will give her citrate of iron and eau de goudron again; and a little time after that, she will begin to gain strength." Who will infuse a little of the energy and life of which I was speaking, into the practice of continental medicine! I wrote down the doctor's plan of treatment, and told him that, having consulted our daughter upon it, she herself said that nothing would cure her but a long sea voyage—that she panted for the sea; and that we were, therefore, about to start in a sailing vessel for the New World. I twice called upon him, and requested him, as his countryman advised me, to send in his bill. I know not if he was

CHAP. I.—BORDEAUX.

annoyed at our cutting short the five months illness he had foretold before convalescence should begin; but he heeded not my request, and we are still his debtors for a few francs.

I doubted not that we should find regular liners, sailing packets, from Bordeaux, the third sea port in France, to New York or some other portion of the United States; and began my enquiries accordingly. Imagine my surprise, when I was told that such were unknown in these waters! Behold me then in a boat, rowing about the broad Gironde, which forms the harbour of Bordeaux, and boarding every vessel that was outward bound to the New World. There were three only! One of them was a little Swedish vessel, which I remember because it was painted green, from the mast head to the keel, and was called by some name which sounded like " The Twistedellen", and which was so small, that I would not go on board; and another from New York, which would sail about a fortnight before I could be ready to go. I asked the captain, if he could not defer his voyage, and he frankly replied: " Well, now; if you make it worth a captain's while not to put to sea, I guess he can always find something in his boat to keep him a week or so longer; but I can't wait a fortnight."

At length, I found a French vessel called the " Belle Assize ", which had been just built by Messrs. Rothschild, and was to start about my time, on her first voyage with a cargo of claret to New Orleans. She was a beautiful vessel, apparently too roomy in her bulk to be a fast sailer; but with excellent accommodation for a few passengers. The officers were a superior class of men, taken from the republican navy; for, in those days, there was a republic with a president in France. New Orleans was not the part at which we wished to land; but as we had planned to spend the next winter at St. Louis, it mattered little whether we should land at New Orleans, and go up the Mississippi; or whether we should reach it from New York, and descend the king of rivers on our return to Europe. The terms were soon agreed upon, and we began our preparations.

I had much difficulty in finding at Bordeaux any modern map of the United States: those which the stationers offered me as most recent, showed only wilds and rivers, where I knew several new states to have been founded; and I wish here to record my thanks to the United States Consul at Bordeaux, who invited me to his rooms, that I might study, as often as I pleased, his great map of the Union; and who gave me much information with frankness and cordiality. It seems familiarly strange to me now, (sitting, as I am, at my window at Leghorn, and overlooking the green Mediterranean,) it seems familiarly strange to me now that little sketch of the Central States of North America which lies beside me in my pocket book, as I then copied it from the consul's map, and could hardly realise the magnitude of the localities I was so soon to travel over!

We had one fatiguing day's work at the French custom house. In order to export our plate from the country, and recover the deposit, (forty-four francs on every kilogramme) which is required on all old English plate brought in for private use, it was necessary that the whole should be verified. Behold then our three chests opened, and their contents laid out on the dressers and tables of the custom house; behold little spoons and great spoons; little forks and great forks; behold knives and dishes and corner dishes and cream ewers and all the apparatus of English breakfast and dinner services, exciting the wonder and the smiles, and sometimes the admiration of the French employés as they sort each kind, and count and weigh it separately to ascertain whether, in number and weight, it corresponds with the receipt given when it entered the country; behold them next count the whole number of pieces together, and weigh them in one lot to see if the totals correspond with their fractional entries; behold them next replace them in the chests and weigh the chests, and then enclose the chests in canvas, cord and seal them with the leaden seal of the Douane, and again weigh them all as they lay ready for the voyage. What a labour it was! However, this was the result, as they entered it in their books: "Three cases, Nos. 16, 20, and 21, weighing together *brut*," that is gross, "229 Kilos—stript 220 Kilos: containing 784 pieces of plate for table, weighing together real net weight 113

Kilos, 132 grammes, all having been used. Summary: brut weight 229; brut, but stript of canvass, 220. Recognised clear weight, 113, 132: 784 pieces." What a labour it was! The conclusion was satisfactory to them, and, what we more cared for, it was satisfactory to us; as we were able to receive again, so soon as they should be certified to be on board with the seals unbroken, the deposit required on entering France.

This, and other matters preparatory to our departure, were comfortably settled, and the agent for the *Belle Assize* brought in the draft of agreement for our passage. In it, was a stipulation that, if the captain should put into any harbour between Bordeaux and New Orleans, the maintenance of my family while there should be at our own cost. I demurred to this clause, and though assured that it was a usual formulary in the French passenger navy, I went to consult my wife upon it. In my absence, the agent and a clerk who accompanied him began talking together; and one of my children came and told me that they were expressing a doubt whether, on account of some delay in the delivery of the cargo, the *Belle Assize* would reach New Orleans before the unhealthy season set in. The dread of the yellow fever flashed upon us! I had not thought it began so soon! I took advantage of the alleged uncertainty as to the time of the vessel's starting; broke off our treaty; and resolved to go to Havre and embark thence for New York. I left some of our luggage to go by way of New Orleans, and this I insured at Bordeaux at the rate of $1\frac{1}{4}$ per cent.; the property, money, plate, and jewels which we took with us, for reasons which will hereafter be stated, I also insured in the same office, to go from Havre to New York in a sailing vessel, at $\frac{1}{2}$ and at $\frac{5}{8}$ per cent. The French are excellent men of business for those who do not grudge the time needed to carry out all their methodical ways; and I found no difficulty in effecting all these arrangements.

Farewell then to Talence. Fourteen weeks of the winter and spring had glided away since we entered the quiet village: they had glided away in such solitude as can be known by a young father and mother surrounded by twelve children—six boys and six girls—of ages varying from two to nineteen. The reader must become acquainted with my children. It was for those boys, that we were about to undertake the voyage to America. From the time of the birth of my second son, I had determined that emigration to the back woods would be the happiest lot for all of them during my life; for all, but the eldest, after me. Fond of a country life myself, I had resolved that the chances of happiness were greater to young men who (first endowed with classical education such as is given in Europe) should occupy lands of their own in the New World, and see their children grow up around them to a similar lot, than they would be to the same young men if harnessed to any of the professions in England, through which they perhaps might, by the time they were sixty, earn a competence on which to marry and breed up another race of aspiring paupers. Right or wrong, this had been my settled conviction through life; and we would now take an opportunity of visiting the country with them and of becoming acquainted with their future home, while our daughters were not old enough to require our residence elsewhere. Three of our sons had already been to some of our best Catholic Colleges in England. Our daughters had worked, like other young ladies, with governesses and masters: and at Talence, education and accomplishments had not been neglected. I had encouraged my children to publish, as we grandiloquently called it in the language of " the Trade", a family periodical once a fortnight, to which each one contributed such thoughts and such caligraphy as he or she could command. One of our daughters was appointed editor of the Bosquet de Flore, as we entitled the journal; and three years and many events that have since chanced, seem to have given sentiment to some doggerel lines that I addressed to her in the first number, and which I will copy here in order to make the reader better acquainted with his future fellow-travellers :

Talence :
A place in France.
Can aught enhance
Its beauties or advance
Its claims to love ?   What blessed chance
Has led us through a weary countrydance

By steamer, railroad, diligence,
To this sweet pilgrimage ? I'd break a lance
With whoso said one word against the manse
We've found in it, and make them elsewhere prance.
But now that I've worn out this rhyming stanz-
-A, let me hail the sweet Bosquet de Flore
In different rhyme. Oh may it more and more
Endure, and sweet and sweeter grow :—a store
Of *souv'nirs* of Talence that o'er and o'er
We may recur to from whatever shore
Shall be decreed to us; and ne'er deplore
Our short stay here nor think it was a bore.
When love and piety are at the core
Of every heart, all earth becomes a floor
From which the buoyant spirit learns to soar
Aloft and knock at heaven's half-open'd door.
In after years, when these are 'days of yore,'
So let us deem of them : and
" ' Heretofore,'
Thus let us say, 'how pleasantly they wore
Away, those weeks at Talence ! Goodness, lore,
And love were ours. Those winter mornings hoar
On which we rose and hasten'd to implore
God's grace at church, are sweet to ponder o'er :—
Though some were left to lie abed and snore.
Oft the high road was red with swinish gore.
Two pigs were kill'd—sometimes they slaughter'd four :
Dogs lapp'd and for the offal fought and tore,
While men look'd on, stuff'd sausages and swore.
At Talence, too, began the 'Bosquet de Flore,'
In which we each put forth our little store
Of wit.'...Dear Louie ! I can write no more.
May the good God thou truly dost adore
Thee prosper—thee and thine for evermore.

Forgive these trifles. Life would be very dry without them : and it is the purport of these pages to describe, not only the travels, but the thoughts, the feelings, the impressions of a family under somewhat novel and trying circumstances.

How the rain poured down on the morning of the 2nd May 1851, when we left our pretty villa of Mr. Crespi and drove through Bordeaux to the port! A guard from the Octroi at Talence accompanied us through the town, lest we should open any of our boxes and scatter eatables or drinkables by the way that had not paid the proper tax. Never have I seen a vessel more crowded than was the little steamer on which we embarked on the broad Gironde. Some two hundred people were choking in a little cabin below deck capable of holding ten in such comfort as cabins below deck afford : but I had not seen the river steamers of the new world, and did not then grumble as memory does now. It continued to rain; and, after two or three hours, we landed at Blaye.

There began the post road through la Vendée to Saumur on the Loire, where it met the railroad to Paris. There was nothing interesting in this road. Few parts of France look attractive to the passing traveller. Saintes, on the Charante, was a pretty-looking place; and they gave us an excellent dinner there for about the same money they had charged at the pot-house at Blaye for an infamous breakfast: but these pages are not to tell of European travel, and I speed me onwards. I would only pause to recommend the Hôtel du Faisan at Tours, and the Hôtel d'Orleans at the latter place. We returned a second time to the Hôtel de l'Amirauté at Havre.

The English Consul at Hâvre was a very gentlemanly man—rather above his place, as most of our *employés* are. The one of Bordeaux had been absent all the winter, and his substitute could only charge heavy fees for the deeds he witnessed for me. Our Consul at Havre did not know what the fees were; but his clerk did, who sat in the ante-room. Said clerk also insisted upon *viséing* my passport, and making me pay for his doing so; but the police assured me that such *visé* was unnecessary. I called on the American Consul, also, at Hâvre : he kept three or four clerks ; but he sat in the same room with them, and came forward and gave me, gratis, all the information I needed, with the willing *prévenance* that I have found more amongst American than any other *employés*. Much of national feeling and national manners may be learnt in the bureaux, whether of government or railway or other companies, in the different States : and those who have travelled enough to understand manner and intonation of the voice as well as spoken words, will probably agree with me that the French of every class, in and out of office, used to evince to us more incivility and ill-manners than any other people in the world. They could not overcome their national antipathies. We shall see what will be the effect of our anti-Russian alliance.

CHAPTER II.

THE KATE HUNTER.

The lapdog—The parrot—The dormouse—The dream—Search for a vessel—The outward bound—Torbay—Life on board—Young Go-a-head—Captain Parsons—Icebergs—Mysterious causes of our mode of travel—Our yacht—Accidents—The pilot—Our invalid.

My eldest son, who had gone from Talence to England to settle some business for us, could not return in time to embark with us. Only eleven of our children, therefore, were to accompany us. But we had as many other pets as Don Juan carried with him from St. Petersburg. We had a lapdog—no great beauty in England, being a cross between a yellow cur and a long-haired spaniel: but as it was small and retained the long hair of one of its progenitors united to the dun colour of the other, it was admired by many people. We had six canary birds in a cage—having given two, of a brood hatched at Talence, to our curé and two to our landlord there. We had an African parrot in a tin travelling box, which I had often joyed to see the French porters, ignorant of its contents, bury under piles of baggage; but the malicious beast would not be smothered, and generally uttered some scream which startled and caused them to release it from its confinement. I own that I had done all I could to cause its neck to be twisted: with the chance of going into Italy, I had taught it to cry " à bas l'Autriche!" " Vive Napoléon!" and I now laboured to make it say " General Cass—hurra!" I fondly hoped that some or other contending faction would silence it for me: but there I now still hear it below stairs—whistling, whooping, and crying " Vive Napoléon!" as if triumphant over me and all its own adventures. We had a dormouse also, with a hairless tail: for said dormouse had a habit of escaping from its box; and being once caught by the tail, it had slipped its skin, which had remained, like a scabbard, in my wife's fingers. She had dreamed a dream about that dormouse, which I submit to the judgment of those curious in such matters. She had dreamed, some three years before, when this dormouse, who was called " Sailor", had a fellow-pet, called " Soldier", that it said to her, " Oh, Mistress, Sailor has beaten me so cruelly that I have been obliged to run away and hide in your box of worsted work." Of course, when the maid came in the morning to wake her mistress, she told her to fetch instantly the dormouse cage. The cage was open: a small spot of blood stained its door—" Sailor" alone was there, and poor injured " Soldier" was missing.

" Fetch the box of worsted !"

In vain it was tumbled over: no dormouse was to be found. Who would be so silly as to believe in dreams!

Three weeks afterwards, a doll's cap was wanted: the worsted box was again hunted over; and there, in a netted cap, used as a bag for loose bits of worsted, was found coiled up the missing dormouse. He was near starved, and had eaten half the worsted around him. All this is a fact. Whether it afterwards died in consequence of Sailor's cruelty, its own escapade or starvation, matters not: but I am happy in being able to record, also as a fact, that, at Hâvre, I had only to take a passage for one dormouse to America!

We walked out along the quays. They were crowded with shipping. Advertisements swang to many of them and declared whither they would sail and when. We came to a fine vessel on which was a similar notice that it would leave Hâvre for New York on the following day. We clomb the staging and went on board.

Now as I had never been on board any vessel before, excepting the two in the harbour of Bordeaux and the channel packets, from the decks of which I had peered down into the cabin beneath without ever venturing to descend the ladder into the close and dingy atmosphere below, I was no less delighted than surprised by the arrangements of the *Kate Hunter*. There was, indeed, a ladder leading to the usual dingy dungeons below deck: but the smart sailor who had received us, led us past this into a spacious saloon built upon the deck itself, and which received plenty of light and air from wide skylights in the ceiling. On each side of this saloon, were five cabins, containing two beds each, and which were lighted by portholes and windows in the side of the building, All were perfectly clean and handsomely fitted up with gilding and painting. From the saloon into which all these opened, two staircases led us up to the roof above them or quarter-deck—a large open space of the size of half the vessel, from one end of which we looked down upon the main deck, sailors, and pitch and tar, about fourteen feet below us.

" When do you sail?"

" To-morrow."

" What passengers have you?"

" Three hundred and sixty German emigrants."

" What cabin passengers?"

" Not one."

" Where is the captain?"

" On shore. I say, Mr. Stubbs," he called to one on deck, " will you have the goodness just to step across the quay to the office, and ask Captain Parsons to come on board."

My wife and I looked at one another as much as to say " this will do."

A tall, sensible-looking man, of about fifty years of age, dressed in black, came on board.

"Captain Parsons, you sail to-morrow. We cannot be ready until the afternoon of the following day."

He did not answer us as frankly as the master of the American vessel at Bordeaux had done; but still he gave us to understand that a captain could always delay his departure for some hours if it were made worth his while to do so.

"We should want all your saloon, and all your state cabins."

This, indeed, looked serious. We began our calculations on either side, and the terms were soon agreed to: provided always that my eleven children were what I represented them to be. Captain Parsons begged me to excuse his American caution, but said that he had once known the captain of a vessel engage to carry and feed an emigrant man and wife and their children, the latter of whom turned out to be as big and about as old as their parents. We appointed him to call upon us at teatime that evening. He did so, and not being frightened by the age, size, or masculine looks of any of our sons or daughters, completed the provisional agreement we had made.

And now much business was to be done, and but one day and a-half remained to do it in. Letters were to be written; codicils to wills and powers of attorney were to be signed; money was to be had from the bank; and little comforts for the sea voyage were to be purchased; physic for the medicine chest; seed for the birds; nuts for the dormouse. We worked hard that day and the following morning. A kindly priest had volunteered to offer up the Holy Sacrifice for our prosperous voyage, and we had all received the Blessed Sacrament, and committed ourselves to the protection of Heaven: then at midday on Wednesday, the 7th of May, we cheerfully stepped on board the *Kate Hunter* from the outermost pier against which it had been towed to receive us. One of our daughters, her arm encumbered with a basket, that necessary appendage to all women travelling, staggered as she mounted the inclined plane up the side of the vessel:—

"Don't be afraid now, miss," said the second mate, who assisted her: "if you were to fall into the sea, I'd bet a dollar we'd soon pick you out again."

"Thank you, but I would rather not try the experiment," she replied, when safe on board.

Another of our children carried the cage of canaries, and, the door not being properly fastened, out flew the mother of the brood, and winged her way back to the streets of the town. Some of us were very sentimental about this separation of the parent bird from her young at the moment of their departure. All, however, were soon busied in arranging their cabins, carpet-bags, and portmanteaus, which I advised them to do while the ship lay in still water. Then the Captain came on board: and then we all went on deck, and saw our vessel towed by a steamer past the wharves crowded with people, many of whom cheered the emigrants as they passed. Those poor emigrants! —how different were the expressions of their countenances! Regret, terror, and hope struggled for the mastery. Many mothers with young children were there, evidently going to rejoin their husbands, and so nerved to the trial they anticipated on their crowded deck. Some fine lads exuberant with joy, triumphed in the anticipation of the future. There were many fathers of families with wives and children, anxious and doubtful, like myself, of the prudence of the course they were taking, and fearful of the dangers into which they might be leading those who confided in their judgment. But it was my wife's birthday; and we all stood about her and were resolved that it should open to us upon a bright future. The children clustered together on deck and sang appropriate songs,—" A health to the outward bound", or " The sea, the open sea". It was well they should sing while they could.

The Captain went coolly and methodically to work. He stood on the lower deck; and calling over the names of all the passengers, made them pass before him. Some objected: but his quiet air of determination quickly showed them that his will was to be obeyed. At last, from the lower decks, they turned out one whose name was not on the register: a stowaway: of course, there was much threatening of what should be done to him; but no one would subscribe to pay his passage. He was placed on a stool, with his hands tied to the rigging over his head, for three hours, and was then turned adrift amongst the crew to work his way out. Our crew was, indeed, a motley set: Germans, Norwegians, Dutch, Irish, and English: sixteen only in number to work a vessel of upwards of one thousand tons. Not an American was amongst them except the Captain, his mate, Mr. Burdock, and his second mate, Mr. Hobbs: and I was surprised to learn that Americans very rarely choose the sea as a profession: never, indeed, unless they have the sure prospect of rising shortly to the command of a vessel. Our second mate, of whom we heard nothing except that he grumbled to my children that the Captain would never carry sail enough to go a-head,—our second mate, " Young Go-a-head", as we called him, was only nineteen, but would doubtless, I was told, be intrusted with the command of a vessel in three years more.

Unless he be calmed down, I would rather not sail in her.

It was wonderful to see how this motley crew of different nations, and of whom many did not speak the language of the others nor of the Captain, was soon brought into order, taught to understand the commands given, and to work together. We were short-handed, it is true; but the bolts used in American rigging are more easily worked than those of English vessels; and we could always, in case of need, find willing help from among the able-bodied emigrants below.

Our songs were interrupted by dinner and by unpleasant sensations; somewhat sadly, we saw the sun set; and nerving myself not to repent our undertaking nor to dread the future, I betook myself, for the first time in my life, to my berth; and went to sleep, wondering how we should get through a whole month in such quarters.

We were awakened next morning by the clear sound of the ship's clock striking two bells. Be it known to landsmen, that the day of twenty-four hours is, on board ship, broken up into three divisions of eight hours each, beginning at midday: that the clock is regularly altered by the sun: but that the bells alone give the recognised time, and that those cannot be struck without superior orders. I rose, washed and dressed, as well as I could in a little space about nine feet long and six feet broad, where ewers and looking-glasses were fixed in such way only as to take up least space,—the floor gently undulating beneath me, and the walls of the room slowly inclining from one to the other side. We all met on deck: the sun was shining brightly: the deep blue sea was spangled by its rays: many fishing boats, with white or brick-coloured sails, were around us: green hills rose in the distance on our right. We were becalmed near Tor Bay.

Tor Bay—Torquay! what pleasant hours I had spent beside that pretty shore! What hopes, what happiness, had sprung to me from that calm retreat! And here we lie and look at it; and the fishing boats supply us with fish; and the vessel sways from side to side on the sunny waves for about eight and forty hours. But then—up arose the breeze, and away we went, westward! There was not much wind, but the effect was disagreeable enough; and we had not much appetite when we were called down to dinner.

" But what is this on the table?" I asked.

" A spider."

Dear landsman, I knew no more than you what " a spider" meant on a dinner-table on board ship: and I lifted up the table cloth to examine the wooden framework which covered it all, and divided it into little boxes, about three inches deep and twelve or more inches wide or long, according to the size of the plates or dishes that were placed upon it. We all admired the contrivance; and still more so when the ship leant on one side, and some plates, that had been set down at the other end of the table beyond the "spider", slid upon the floor, while our own dishes were firmly fixed in its fangs.

Captain Parsons had engaged to supply us with all proper provisions as state-room passengers; but he had so short a time to lay in stores, that I was somewhat anxious as to how we should fare. My wife had requested him to take on board a goat to supply us with fresh milk, which we all found more agreeable than the so-called preserved milk in tins. The preserved meats, however, which he took for us—the salmon, sardines and tunny in oil—were excellent. Of poultry there was a good store, though the ducks pined for want of water to swim in. Fresh butcher's meat of course disappeared after the first few days, and the eggs were no longer new laid: but the broiled ham was plentiful and good; and by living very sparingly on this, on currys, on preserved fish, with pickle and vinegar, I managed to keep off all positive sea sickness, and suffered only from the nasty nausea which I imagine to be inseparable from salt water. Then we had hot rolls, half baked according to the universal practice in America, and corn bread in abundance. This latter was not unpleasant, but too sweet for my palate. I was glad to see that my children liked it. Our dinners were always at two o'clock: our breakfasts we persuaded our host to defer till near eight o'clock: and our teas were at seven.

Fried and cold ham, and lots of omelets; with hot rolls and corn bread; with tea and coffee and fried potatoes, made these meals ample for those even of our party to whom the sea breeze gave most appetite. The Captain sat at the head of the table: his first mate next to our boys at the bottom; and as yet unused to the American plan of bolting their food, we marvelled how the latter could get through his meals and be again on deck before we had well nigh begun ours. The Captain's evident wish to conform to our ways, could not make even him sit what we thought a decent time at the board: and he always stole away on deck and smoked his one segar after every meal before we were ready to rejoin him.

My poor wife, although the only one of the party who had been much at sea, and generally without sickness, suffered greatly on this voyage. She struggled against it at first, but then fairly gave in, and spent most of her mornings in her state room. The children, according to their different constitutions and the thoughtlessness or energy of their characters, suffered or escaped all ailing. The younger ones generally disregarded the nuisance: they eat, and were ill, and got well again, and played about and enjoyed the novelty of the scenes around them. Our invalid suffered least from sea sickness, and gained strength visibly in the fresh salt breeze. She was always up early on deck before breakfast, and soon acquired a tolerable footing on its heaving floor. She enjoyed carrying cups of tea or coffee to her mother's room, and showing that she could do so without spilling their contents, when, as she said, the ship " raised her bows to allow the wave to pass under her without splashing her face, or figure-head". Our eldest daughter looked after and tended all in their ailings and wants: our little Isabel amused the youngest children, and constituted herself their day nurse: the one and the other were often sick; but silently rushed away and eased themselves, and then returned to their self-appointed duties with good nature and smiles as if nothing had happened. The boys ran wild, and pretended that they were learning navigation. At nightfall, we all collected round the table in the saloon, and studied together the American books or atlases belonging to the Captain,—in which, to our surprise, America was described first in endless district and county maps, while Europe was left to the end of the volume, and dismissed with scarcely one for each kingdom :—we studied the maps, and fancied a home for our boys in the different states, and sketched and discussed plans of houses to be built for each, with one in the centre of the location for us all to inhabit when we came to visit them, and which should always be transmitted to the head of the colony. Vain dreams, but pleasant! Where are now all those who strove for the unbuilt room which imagination allotted to each! Their lot has been already otherwise cast. But never were more cheerful castles in the air more innocently built: and never did young hearts anticipate the gaieties and crowds of a festive capital, as ours looked forward to a patriarchal home in the wildernesses of the back woods!

On—on we went, pleasantly and rapidly too. We were delighted with the behaviour of our vessel, which, in a few hours, overtook and passed everything that we came in sight of. My wife insisted that the masts were too tall, and that she must fall over on one side : and was scarcely reconciled by Captain Parsons' assurance that American ships were so built for greater speed than Europeans could attain. Young "Go-a-head", indeed, still grumbled to my boys that we did not carry sail enough : but the captain was a prudent man ; and greater watchfulness could not be than he evinced in the sailing of his boat. I do not believe that, while the sun was above the horizon, he was ever more than half an hour from the wheel; and when the wind was at all high, he never left it, even during the night.

For the wind was high sometimes ; and it was with an unpleasant sensation that we all woke one morning and found ourselves standing up in bed, either on our feet or on our heads, or lying across the portholes in the side, or rolling on the floors of our state-rooms ; while towels and looking-glasses, that we had left hanging in all the proprieties of matter well taught to obey the centre of gravity,

CHAP. II.—THE KATE HUNTER.   51

seemed flying off in an eccentric course, their lower extremities far-stretching from the wall. It was no easy matter to dress and shave that morning. When I had accomplished the task, and had been released from my state-room, against the door of which something had rolled, I sadly wanted sea-legs to cross the saloon and go on deck. I had got half way across, and was greeting our captain as he entered from the slips on the opposite side, when the ship gave what, I suppose, was an unusual lurch; for not only was I hurled back to my cabin-door, but the captain himself staggered, and was thrown somewhat roughly beside me. I was told, however, that this was no storm, but only a stiff breeze that was carrying us on favourably. And on, I suppose, we went, and off too: as some of my children, who were lying on sofas round the saloon, occasionally found themselves gently deposited on the floor and rolling under the breakfast table. Yet even this brought its fun; for my third boy, Frank, soon discovered that tea, spilt from his own cup, could be made to run across the sloping table into the lap of his sister opposite; and, of course, did not neglect this opportunity of improving his knowledge of hydraulics.

" When I went on deck," writes our invalid, " I was struck with the majestic, perhaps awful grandeur of the sight. There was not another ship to be seen, and we were alone on the wide Atlantic, dashing through the waves. The sky was dark and lowering, and the wind whistled through the masts and spars."

Such was the impression, produced on the mind of a young girl of sixteen, by a stiff breeze at sea; and such, I believe, must be its effect on all :—the loneliness of the ship we are on and the immensity of the ocean, contrast predominantly. But the breeze subsided and was followed by a calm; and the *Kate Hunter* rolled disagreeably; and then a fair breeze sprang up; and then it changed and carried us rather too far to the north: and then we, who were sailing on the great circle, found the air grow chill for the month of May; and one morning when it was getting rather unpleasantly cold, they called down to us that three large icebergs were in sight. The sick forgot their sickness, and speedily all were on deck. How steadily they floated by us, those great mounds of snow! Not "mountains high", as imagination fancies icebergs to be; but like small islands of snow-covered ice, large enough to whelm the largest vessel with which they should come in contact, they seemed to go on their way rejoicing towards the sun—rollicking and turning from side to side as one portion melted away in its rays and another sank deeper into the water: —and be it remembered that the part covered by the water is always two-thirds larger than that which appears above. At one time, we had about a score of these in sight, and not far from us. A large bird with black wings visited us from one of these islands, and hovered around our spars. We thought of the albatross of the "Ancient Mariner", and bid heaven speed it on its way: but we were not sorry to incline again to the south, and to pass out of the course of such fearful neighbours.

And so our days went by, as pleasantly as days can go by on board ship. Had the *Kate Hunter* been a private yacht, she could not have sailed better, nor have been better manned and kept;

nor could we have had it more entirely to ourselves. The poor emigrants never, of course, interfered with our saloon or deck, and caused us no annoyance whatever. The mate told us to congratulate ourselves that they were Germans rather than Irish, or that we might have been sensible of their vicinity. Irishmen—Irishwomen! why will you compel a well-wisher to you and your country to hear such a reproach against you from those who had no ill-will to you or yours? It was distressing to be confined so long with upwards of three hundred people, in whose histories and hopes one could have felt interest and sympathy, without holding any communication with them; but I could not find out that any one of them spoke any language but their own; and as they all had their own bedding and provisions and cooked their own meals, little need of intercourse was there between them and the crew of the vessel. All that Captain Parsons knew of them was, that they had been brought from Germany to Hâvre by an Emigration Company, who had there chartered his vessel to take them to New York.

Sunday and other Sundays came round; and we used to stand in groups on the deck or hang over its rails as we read the Divine Service for the day, while the captain walked his quarter-deck on the other side and would not even gambol with the lapdog until the books were closed: but he soon found out that the afternoon service was less rigidly formal, and as my children clustered together and sang the Vesper psalms to the old church music, he would stand near and listen with a pleased expression, or trip away with Tiny snapping at his heels, while he dragged our youngest two-year-old boy by the hand beside him and played with him *sotto voce*. He was a kind-hearted man, well informed, with good manners and obliging; and evidently felt much interest in our large family going so far under such unusual circumstances. For English gentlemen's sons do not often go out to settle in the United States; and when they do, they are not accompanied by father and mother and sisters and young children, all speeding from the luxuries of wealth and social position, that they may "rough it" unknown in the sailing vessel or the wilderness; and may so become acquainted with the future home of their sons and brothers. There were also other mysterious circumstances about the party which Captain Parsons could never fathom, and which must yet remain unrevealed to the reader.

A sea voyage is said to be tedious; but to a family afloat for the first time, it can never be without its excitement and incidents. How interesting it was to hear captain and mate, with spyglass in hand, speculate upon the identity of some vessel miles ahead—certain only that she was European because of the heaviness of her build and rigging—and break off the useless speculation, saying, " It matters not: we shall pass her shortly!"—What pleasure it was then to feel that we were parties interested in the character of our pretty *Kate Hunter*, and to watch her stealing along the waters and gaining—gaining, till, in three hours, we passed the other, and recognised her as one that had left Hâvre a fortnight before ourselves! How amusing it was to note the gambols of the dolphins which sometimes used to cover the sea like floating weeds—to mark them heaving their round glittering backs far above the blue wave, and then roll and tumble over as if they enjoyed the cool bathing and the power of swimming in it while the sun shone so bright over head! How exciting it was to be startled from our reading round the saloon lamp at night, by one of the boys, who had escaped on deck, rushing down and calling to us that the sea was on fire! Then how blissful to hang over the sides of the vessel and mark the bright phosphoric gleaming in the track of the rudder and around and on every side on the dark face of the ocean, whenever a tiny wave toppled over its surging crest, as if silver and gold sands were flashing up from beneath! The sky over head was a deep dark blue, through which millions of stars brightly shone. A light wind was gently swelling out the white sail that hung from our tapering spars; and onwards, almost without motion, onwards glided our wedge-like clipper, as silent as the stars above or the ocean around; onwards into those bright phosphoric waves in front, and leaving a broad track of liquid flashes over the dark blue sea behind her.

And then, too, we had our broils and incidents of human life. Our German steward and the cook would often disagree; and once in their quarrels they issued forth where we could see them on the emigrant's deck; and the steward caught up a carving knife and was making towards his foe, when out rushed Captain Parsons, who seemed to be everywhere at once, and began silently to belabour the steward with a rope that he caught up. I promise you that the German bore on his person for many days the marks of that rope's-ending. Flogging is forbidden on board the merchant navy of the United States; but no captain hesitates to inflict it when he thinks necessary; and public opinion prevents the culprit from declaring his own ill-conduct by informing against the law-breaker.

One day, in crossing the deck, one of our emigrants fell and broke his leg. Captain Parsons was instantly there, and having caused the poor man to be laid upon a stretcher, he himself set the limb and bound it with splinters in a manner which, as I afterwards heard, was satisfactory to the surgeon on shore. We had no surgeon on board the *Kate Hunter;* and subsequent experience of him of the *Asia* steamer inclines me to exonerate those who chartered the vessel from the omission. Two poor little babies were born on board about this time; I know not if with our captain's assistance.

A tidy lass from amongst the emigrants acted as our stewardess, and fulfilled her duties with alacrity and cheerfulness; and the more so when, seeing the crucifix in one of our cabins, she exclaimed "Catolische!" and joyfully crossed herself to show that there was sympathy of faith between us. More than that, our daughters could not understand; but this was a bond of benevolence.

But now the colour of the sea began to change from dark blue to green; and a sparrow alighted upon our deck and brought us news of land. Poor little thing! it seemed very faint; and when, with thoughts of the "Ancient Mariner's" albatross, I divined that it must be thirsty and fetched a glass of water and poured it out on the deck, it hopped into it and sipped deliciously. It was unable to eat the crumbs we scattered until it had taken many a swallow of the fresh water. Hopping about the rigging, it stayed with us some hours, and then we saw it no more.

We had been becalmed several days since we started; and, on the 31st of May, being then one hundred and thirty miles from New York, were again lying idle, whistling for a wind. The sun had risen very bright and warm; the sky was a deep unclouded blue; many vessels were in sight becalmed like ourselves. The captain and mate were very busy with their glasses; and, at length, distinguished a small open boat which had put off from the side of a vessel on the nature of which they had differed. This settled the question. By degrees, we were able to distinguish the six rowers who urged the little boat over the heaving sea; and after three hours' hard work, it came alongside of us and a pilot climbed on deck.

Few words were interchanged between him and the captain—men of business both; when the latter gave up the command of his vessel, and joyfully went down to his cabin to study the bundles of newpapers which had just been handed to him. The pilot had been for the last three days lying in wait at this distance from land, on the look out for some vessel that he might take into harbour. A hard life that!

But we were not yet at the end of our voyage. All that day, and the next, we lay becalmed with our pilot on board. Our feelings were divided between the restlessness of *ennui* at being detained so near shore, and the fear lest we should be carried into harbour during the night, and so lose the first sight of "the land of the brave and the free", as our captain now—feeling that, like Rob Roy, he "stood upon his own land, and his name was Mac Gregor"—boastfully called it.

"Next morning," writes Lucy, our invalid, in the memoranda of her travels, from which I copy, "next morning, I woke with a start, fearing that I had slept too long. It was four o'clock: and looking out of my little window, I saw the golden sun shining on land. My first feeling was gratitude to God for having preserved us during this long voyage: and I knelt down and thanked Him who had watched over us; and whom I thought that I, of all, ought more particularly to thank. For when I first went on board the *Kate Hunter*, I had felt that I should either die during the voyage (and had prepared myself to die), or that I should get well and strong; and I now prayed that I might be of some use to my parents, who, I felt and knew, would require all their children's help in the travels we were about to undertake. I then dressed myself, and went on deck. It was a beautiful sight to one who had not seen land for three weeks. Long Island was on our right hand, and Staten Island, so I was told they were called, was on our left. Numbers of ships, boats, and steamboats of all kinds were on the water, which was beautifully blue, but not like the blue of the middle of the ocean. I repeated the *Te Deum* as all this met my sight."

Having left Havre in the afternoon of the 7th of May, and cast anchor in the night of the 1st and 2nd of June, we had made the voyage out in twenty-five days: not bad sailing, considering that we had been becalmed five or six.

CHAPTER III.

NEW YORK.

Quarantine.—The custom house officer.—Irish carmen and porters.—Our children on board.—Broadway.—American omnibuses.—The post office.—The money changer.—Speculation.—The cobler.—Hotels.—Gentle and simple.—A chambermaid.—Private rooms.

I HAD often heard the harbour of New York compared to the Bay of Naples; and I can now testify that both are formed of land and water. Other resemblance, I saw not: nothing whatever on which to found any degree of comparison. The grand distinguishing feature of New York harbour is the variety and freshness of its waters; uncrowded, unencumbered by a mass of various shipping, such as would block up any other port in the world. But where does New York harbour begin?—where end? Is it the mouth of a river, or is it an inlet of the sea amongst headlands, adown which a navigable river flows, and the tide rises some forty miles? an inlet confined between banks from one to five miles apart! To compare this with any mere haven or basin for shipping, were an absurdity.

I did not note that peculiar clearness in the atmosphere of which many English travellers write,—probably because I had been accustomed to the brighter skies of Provence and the South of Europe; but I could not but relish the extraordinary freshness of the scenery around. Woods, hills, houses and churches that dotted them,—all seemed delightfully clean and fresh,—new and not yet worn and soiled by time; and the slim pinnaces and steamers that cut across, rather than through, the waters in every direction, with a speed unknown in the old world, gave to the whole an animation and life such as I had noted in no other scenery.

We were anchored opposite " Quarantine Ground",—which, I was told, was the name of a large building on the shore a quarter of a mile on our left: and the mate had told our boys how, in the early settlement of the country, the beautiful island on which it stands had been purchased from the Indians for an old red uniform coat and six muskets. We had scarcely finished breakfast, when the doctor came on board. He was a fat little man, and joining Captain Parsons, put his questions with the rapidity of routine, but in a tone of natural good humour.

"Well, how are all here? all well? all well?" he asked. "Is that lad hump-backed?" pointing to my fourth son.

"Sit up, my man!" said Captain Parsons, giving him a slap on his rounded shoulders; and the doctor was quickly satisfied that the great republic was not called upon to admit any deformity.

"And in the steerage," he inquired; "how many dead?"

"None."

"How many born?"

"Two."

"Any sickness?"

"None."

"Any deformed,—unable to gain their living?"

"None?"

"Any broken bones?"

"One."

They went to inspect the poor fellow whose leg had been broken on board; and it was explained to me, that, had any of the emigrants been maimed, the captain would have been required to deposit a fund to meet any expense the township might incur in their maintenance. I was also assured, that the fees paid to this doctor of quarantine had so much increased with the increase in the shipping of New York, as to make his place the very best in the Union. I will not venture to record figures: but the remuneration seemed to be preposterously great—some £50,000 sterling a year. The fees of the United States consul at Liverpool in the first six months of that year had been £8000 sterling.

Our captain went on shore, he said, to fetch a custom-house officer, who should examine our luggage on board. This appeared a convenience, and we assented to await his return, while all our packages should be got up from the hold and laid in the saloon. Meanwhile, also, our poor emigrants dressed themselves in their best clothes, and brought up their trunks, on which they seated themselves. They sat for hours, casting wistful eyes on the green land of promise, in which each hoped for plenty or fortune. We went to dinner; and, at three o'clock, an officer came from the customs to examine all personal luggage. Captain Parsons invited him to enter, and take a glass of wine at our table; but he answered that he would dismiss all the emigrants first. Three hundred and sixty of these had, at least, as many boxes: and one man was to inspect them all, and let them go on shore that night! It may well be conceived that the examination was not a very rigid one. Some of the boxes were chalked without being opened at all; many were unlocked and closed after a passing glance at the boots and shoes and working clothes of the owners; some were more rigidly inspected; but, in two or three hours, all were scored with chalk and declared free to land.

This jewel of a custom-house officer then entered our saloon; and as we were having tea, he sat down and took a cup, instead of the wine which he had deferred. Meanwhile, he looked us over, and doubtless formed his own opinion as to our smuggling propensities. He took my four-year-old boy on his knee and chatted with him; then jumping up, said to him, " Come, my little fellow, you come round with me and tell me what is in every one of these boxes."

" A capital device," I said; " children and fools speak truth."

He smiled in reply; and then commenced his tour with the child, who replied to his mock investigation.

" Well now, sir," he said, turning to me, " here are forty-two packages. I shall open four of them. Be so good as to point out which they shall be."

I requested him to make the selection himself. He unlocked two instead of four out of the lot, and then scored them all with chalk and wished us good evening.

The man was evidently above receiving a bribe, like Italian doganieri in all the pride of military uniform; and nothing of the sort was offered to him. He had the good sense to act upon the rational, rather than the vexatious interpretation of the instructions he had received. Let travellers in Europe say which system is the pleasantest, and, in the long run, the most profitable to the revenue of the country—making allowance for the salary of the host of officials whom such an arrival would employ in Europe. The doctor and this customhouse officer had been on board, and we were now free to land with all our goods, and to circulate or reside without hindrance or inquiry, without passport or *carta di soggiorno*, through all and in all the wide territories of the Union!

I inquired what would become of our fellow-emigrants; and was assured that Germans never came unprovided: that each had doubtless his destination fixed before he left his own country—probably in Wisconsin, which is being much settled by Germans—where friends were expecting him; and that assuredly all had sufficient sums of money secreted about their persons, although they seldom "broke bulk" in New York.

At seven o'clock, all our luggage was dragged into a kind of steam-tug, that had come

CHAP. III.—NEW YORK.

alongside our *Kate Hunter*; those of the emigrants who were still on board descended to it; their children were passed down, like so many bales of goods, while the anxious mothers looked on from above or received them in the boat below. Then, with my wife and eldest boy, I also went on it; and, at seven o'clock, we put off from our good ship which had borne us so far and so well. But here I have to record my only complaint against Captain Parsons; here I must record that he behaved ill. He had agreed to take me and my goods in his *Kate Hunter* to New York. He deposited us in a steam-tug five miles from the quay: he did this that he might avoid the expense of harbour dues and await another cargo where he then lay. The consequence was great danger of shipwreck during this short passage; doubtless our insurance, if not our lives, would have been forfeited if it had occurred. I might have protested and required the fulfilment of his contract; but I knew not to what my condescension exposed me.

For, having made our way with some difficulty to the quay through the other barges that lay around it, we were in the midst of a scene of confusion that beggars all description. Scores of trucks and of one-horse carts encumbered the wharf, and others rushed down upon it regardless of those before them. All were owned by Irishmen—the only porters in the United States: and the vociferations, the howls, the curses became terrific. Let me record that I had only heard one oath on board the *Kate Hunter*—that one was hurled by the first mate against the stupidity of one of his crew. What, then, must the Americans think of the fearful swearing of these emigrants! Darkness was coming on:—darkness closed around us: yet there were we confined, hour after hour, while these porters quarrelled among themselves and refused to give way the one to the other. One by one the emigrants leapt on shore, dragging their trunks after them; a few would join together and load a cart with their goods, and think they should, at least, get clear of the throng. Vain hope! A stupid blackguard porter, who had not succeeded in loading his own truck, blocked the

CHAP. III.—NEW YORK. 73

way; and neither cajolery, oaths, nor entreaties could persuade him to move on one side and allow the others to pass. In vain I urged the others to knock him down and drive his horse away: they refused to exercise Lynch law—knowing, I presume, that they were as likely to act in the same manner themselves on the following day: and the swearing and the vociferation went on.

Meanwhile, I had engaged two carts to convey my baggage, and part of it had been landed and piled upon the wharf, when a cry came to me that the steam-tug was sinking, and that they were putting it back into the harbour in order to turn it and bring the heavy-laden side against the pier. This was not a pleasant operation to note through the darkness, while my wife and child were on it and that rabble crowd was howling around me. It was, however, performed in safety; and, at length, our whole baggage was landed and placed upon carts: at length, also, we got clear of the mob on the quay and made our way out. No constable nor policeman had interfered. Why should the citizens of New

E

York tax themselves and support a police to maintain order amongst emigrants and Irish porters? Let them fight it out amongst themselves. A shrewd policy, perhaps: but not a liberal nor a creditable one. Meanwhile I had received my first impression, which every subsequent week confirmed, that the Irish servants and porters (and none but Irish fill such offices in the hotels), that Irish servants and porters were the nuisance of the United States. Despised by the Americans; themselves despising the blacks; with their bellies full for the first time in their lives; insolent in their looks; extortionate in their demands; oaths in their mouths; free from all restraint of neighbourhood or parish priest; beggars upon horseback, they ride full tilt to.... Enough for the present. I would commit them to their clergy and the treadmill.

The porters whom I had selected, of course professed themselves scandalized by the conduct of their brethren: but I was in no humour to listen to their self-laudation: and only urged them to conduct us to the nearest respectable hotel;—I cared not which, so that it were near at hand. They stopped, therefore, in a few minutes, at the door of one which they recommended by the name of the Battery Hotel; the only one, they said, that was at that end of the town. It was half-past ten o'clock when the luggage was deposited in the passage: and we were conducted up a carpeted staircase. The house had altogether an English look. We had a not very comfortable tea in what seemed to correspond with the salle à manger of a French hotel: but my wife wanted only repose: and was much pleased with the look of the large handsomely-furnished bedroom they gave us on the first floor. And so we slept for the first time on the continent of America.

Let us return on board our vessel. "That morning," writes Louie, "I was up before any of my sisters, and was exhausting a superabundance of high spirits by racing over the deck after Tiny the dog, when, to my surprise, I saw two of our brothers mounting the side of the ship from a boat, accompanied by the captain. Frank, the eldest of the two, then told me, as a profound secret, that they had accompanied Captain Parsons on shore, where he had bought some fresh fish, some nice bread (a rather scarce article on board), and some strawberries. I do not think we ever enjoyed a breakfast so much as this, our last on board the *Kate Hunter.*"

" At length," continues Agnes, " we discovered papa and mama pushing towards us in an open boat; we exchanged a hail, and, for the next half hour, we were employed in finishing to pack up, though we had been told to have all ready; but, as usual, something was to be done at the last minute; however, in half-an-hour, all the state rooms had been searched over for the fourth time, each of which was to have been the last, and we all proceeded on deck. Here each of us was tied in a chair, covered with the flag which we were to wrap round us; it was something like being in a swing; and when the signal was given, we were each of us hoisted up into the air over the side of the vessel. With some of us, the leg of the chair caught in the tackle outside the ship, which caused us to be crooked and doubled up in a not very pleasant predicament while it was being freed: then we were let down, quite giddy, into a small boat, which was in great agitation on the waves. The water was unusually rough that morning. There was some doubt how my two youngest brothers could be brought down; but the second mate, young 'Go-a-head', caught them both in his arms, and, seating himself in the chair, deposited them in safety amongst us. But the waves dashed into the boat; and the boatman found out he had made a mistake, when he said it would hold us all. He was obliged to leave our two elder brothers for a second trip. In ten minutes we arrived at the land, but not before some of us were drenched with salt water; however, we little minded it, so glad were we to be on *terra firma* again."

A few turns on the platform dried off the spray of the sea; the rest of our party were put on shore; in ten minutes, the little *Sylph* steamer, that plied between some place lower down and New York, touched at Quarantine platform; we seated ourselves in its ample saloon, built above deck; and soon stepped from it to the quay at New York: "which was very easily done," writes Agnes, "the steamers all being made to join the land, so that you had but to walk on, and would not know the difference, or which was which." This was true; no visible fissure or inequality dividing the floating deck from the platform.

The post-office, the bankers, the money-changers, the railway-offices had to be visited; and the course of business took me over a good part of New York that morning. I have, however, little to describe. Broadway, that we have all heard of, can scarcely be called a handsome street. It seemed to be about two-thirds the width of Oxford Street. It may be, like Oxford Street, three miles long or more; but no one ever spoke of the beauty of Oxford Street. The buildings on each side of Broadway were even more irregular Tall, well-built houses stood beside others half their height; houses of cement stood beside others of rough red or yellow bricks, or beside Stewart's store of white marble—the handsomest shop in the world. The pavement was very bad, if paved it was; but the surface was so uneven, that it was difficult to ascertain whether all really was stone under the dry dirt that covered it. I saw not the pigs usually described as roaming in Broadway; they had been exiled by a recent mayor; perhaps the street would have been cleaner had such scavengers been left to work it. The shops had more the appearance of wholesale warehouses, than of the smart places of retail to which we are accustomed in Europe; and goods, piled outside the doors, or lifted to or from heavy drays, often encumbered the pavement. Where Broadway passes beside the Park,—a triangular space planted with trees, but containing only eleven acres,—the effect is rather fine. But neither here nor elsewhere in the city are there any public buildings that would attract the notice of a travelled European.

The other streets of the city are laid out at right angles to one another, even in the old parts, on the tongue of land between the confluence of the East River and the Hudson; and higher up in the more modern part of the town, they are built by rule and compass, and known to Americans by names denoting the order in which they occur, from First Street to Thirtieth, or it may be, by this time, Sixtieth Street. I marvel how any one can remember so monotonous, so little marked a nomenclature.

A striking feature of New York is the number of new houses that are being erected in every part of it. The pavement was really encumbered, every twenty yards, with piles of bricks and building materials; and they seem to be pulling down one quarter of the town, for no other purpose than that of rebuilding it.

But amid all this disorder of business on a large and flourishing scale, what a racket, what a crowd, what a rush! Hackney-coaches, omnibuses, and carts are driven at such a rate, that my wife insisted the people must be all mad. No handsome equipages, no private carriages, arrest attention in the streets; nor are the lumbering hackney-coaches (whose fare is so high as to preclude their being often used) numerous; but the place seems to swarm with carts, drays, and omnibuses. These, too, are for service rather than for show. New

CHAP. III.—NEW YORK. 81

York cannot afford two men to wait upon each omnibus. The driver has to perform the part of conductor and guard also; and this he is cleverly enabled to do. An open window behind him enables those in the inside to tell him when they wish to get out; they pass their fare through the window to him; he pulls a cord which, working on pullies, opens the door at the tail of the vehicle, and he scarcely checks his horses while the party walks out. Meanwhile, should a passenger, who has not passed his fare through the window in the roof, seize the opportunity and try to escape, the driver pulls the cord again, slams to the door, and catches him by the leg. If people have not their change ready when they wish to get down, it is their own fault, and he carries them on. He may not delay his other passengers and stop the omnibus while they are fumbling for their money.

The weather was very hot; and the men in the streets were mostly dressed in brown linen frock coats. The ladies were much smarter; and selected such glowing colours as they thought best suited to their own complexions.

Scarlet and yellow and the brighter hues seemed most in vogue—the general style of female dress being an exaggeration of Parisian fashions.

At the post office, I found a very inconvenient custom to prevail; the direction of letters addressed to the post office, or to persons whose address is not known, is printed and hung up outside the window for a certain number of days; if not called for within that time, the letters are destroyed. I am surprised that a commercial community, whose correspondence must be so dependent upon winds and waves, should tolerate so clumsy a contrivance for lessening the work of clerks. Very many more letters arrive in either the London, the Liverpool, or the Southampton post office than in that of New York; but it is not found necessary to resort to such a barbaric plan to prevent accumulation.

I was recommended to Mr. Beebee, the money-changer; and a most respectable gentleman I found Mr. Beebee in his little cellar in Wall Street. I consigned to him a large sum in Bank of England notes, for which he gave me a memorandum, allowing for them their fair value and interest, unless he heard by return of post from England that they were forged! We smiled at this symptom of the habits and experience of men of business in New York. But a New York man of business could not willingly see so large a sum of presumed-to-be-genuine money carried beyond his reach without attempting to get something more out of it than what he could make over and above the six per cent. interest he was to allow us for the deposit: and thus the conversation was carried on:—

" Well, sir; I guess you'll make some stay in New York city?"

" No; we purpose leaving it to-morrow or next day."

" Going to Boston or Baltimore and Washington?"

" To neither; we shall go up to the Lakes and into the Far West!"

" What! not remain to see our first-rate seaboard cities?"

" Every city must be more or less alike; and I can judge of the peculiarities of those of your old States by what I see of New York. I know almost every city of Europe: and I think I shall be better able to study America and American character in the country."

" Well, sir; but this money. I can tell you of a mode of investing it here so that it will be surely doubled before you want to call for it. Some coal mines have lately been discovered so placed that we shall be able to drive all competition out of New York. The shares are now low; but, in a few days, will be at a premium. Let me introduce you to my friend here who will give all particulars."

The friend thereupon held out his hand, shook mine with warmth, and began talking with a frankness that, in Europe, could have only sprung from lengthened acquaintance. I observed this throughout the United States: Americans are formal and distant till introduced—it matters not by whom; but that ceremony having once taken place, they break off whatever they might be saying to shake hands, and seem to consider you, thenceforth, as one of themselves.

Mr. Beebee gave me maps and prospectuses

of the coal mine, which he urged me to study and distribute when I should have first secured for myself as many shares as could be bought with the money I had deposited with him; and his friend insisted on taking me to the office of the young company, where I was shown great maps of the mines on the scale of about a yard to a mile. I was very polite; promised to think the matter over; and proceeded on my way; admiring this first specimen of American smartness.

I met Captain Parsons in the street, and he took me into a little shop, hung with white and pink glazed calico, and in the centre of which was a clean counter and half a dozen bottles of wine or spirit, and insisted upon treating me to my first glass of American liquor. What would I have? " Sherry cobler", " mint julip", or a " brandy smasher", — or any of half a dozen other delicacies which he named? I chose the far-famed sherry cobler, and curiously watched the lad behind the counter squeeze a little lemon into a large tumbler full of small lumps of bright, transparent ice; lay over them one or two bits of lemon peel (perhaps a dusting of spice, I am not certain now), cover the whole over with pounded white sugar and then pour about a wine-glassful of sherry over all. He handed it to me with a glass tube about eight inches long. I was shown how to push this among the lumps of ice to the bottom and to suck up through it the liquor there. I did so. The day was excessively hot and I was fatigued by my walk and by my exertions in fighting shy of Mr. Beebee's coal mine. I sucked it up to the last drop: then, turning to Captain Parsons, I exclaimed, " It is worth a voyage to New York to enjoy that!" I did not tell him it was worth what we had undergone on the pier owing to his breach of contract; and we parted good friends.

I need not in future describe the composition of these American drinks. All are made in the same manner; but flavoured differently with mint, brandy, or otherwise. They are very delicious.

There was a large, handsomely furnished sitting-room, with a piano, in our hotel for the use of all the inmates; all were expected to take their meals together in the dining-room. To this we were summoned by a tremendous gong, that rumbled through all the house at one o'clock. When we entered the room a few minutes after, the company had already advanced far through their meal. Vegetables, lobster-salads, and dessert were on the table; the solid meats and the "fruit pies" (elsewhere, open tarts) were carved by the landlord at a side table. No one drank wine or beer, but vast quantities of water, in which floated lumps of ice. "At seven o'clock next morning," writes Louie, "this gong was carried round to the doors of all the bed-rooms, to awaken, and then deafen, all the inmates. In half-an-hour, just as our ears were beginning to recover from the infliction, it was repeated to announce the first breakfast. In another half-hour, the gong sounded again for the second breakfast, consisting of what was left from the first; this meal was for the nurses, children, and all those who had been too lazy to get up in time for the first; the master of the hotel and his family also breakfasted at it. As soon as it was over, all the waiters of the hotel sat down. Throughout America there are no private parlours in the hotels, but two public sitting-rooms: one is called the 'Ladies' sitting-room', the other is a reading-room where the gentlemen smoke and read the papers. Every ladies' room is provided with rocking-chairs. At first we greatly disliked these rocking-chairs, but we soon began to feel differently towards them. The American ladies rock and fan themselves incessantly, except when they play on the piano, one of which is in every sitting-room."

"One day," continues Agnes, "a fat old lady, who seemed glued to the rocking-chair, for we found her there in the morning and left her there at night, pulled towards her the corner of my pocket-handkerchief, and pointing to the mark, said, 'That proves you are from the old country; we could not afford to spend our time in marking things here'. I suppose," continues my saucy child, "it would hinder them from going a-head fast enough. So the churches in this place are obliged to be shut except during service, because some of the New Yorkers, not satisfied with going a-head in the usual manner, would do it by quicker means,—by such as would be called stealing 'in the old country', but which are perhaps justified by liberty and equality here." I deny my child's imputation of dishonesty in the Americans; she was only thirteen when she was in the country—fourteen when she wrote; it may be necessary to close the churches against the emigrants in New York, the riff-raff of Europe; but real Americans must not be confounded with these. "The sun was excessively hot," continues my critic, "so that we did not attempt to see the town in the morning. About five o'clock, a great many parties of very finely-dressed ladies drove in their carriages to the Battery Gardens, under the windows of our hotel, and got out and walked. We went to the Broadway, which is a very handsome street. We noticed a great many pretty girls walking about: many of them in bright scarlet shawls. It was quite astonishing to see the number of houses being built. Parts of almost every street you went into were blocked up with bricks and mortar. Some of the shops in Broadway were very magnificent. There was a linen-draper's shop faced with pillars of white marble; but as people in trade are the gentlemen of America, this is, of course, not to be wondered at; and the more you go west, the more gentle they become; so that, at last, a shoemaker desired a waiter ' to ask the gentleman in the bar to give the man (meaning papa) his boots.'

"The next morning," she continues, " was the commencement of our troubles. Our dear mama had caught cold and over-fatigued herself in landing, and now kept her bed, with a cough, and a blister on her chest. Our pets also began to diminish: our dormouse died, we believe from eating biscuit that had been wetted with the salt water that had washed over us in the boat; and, the same day, one of the canaries was found dead in the bottom of its cage. Our little dog had been ailing for some time on board the *Kate Hunter ;* but its fate was reserved."

" The second night after our arrival at the hotel," Louie records, " mama had rung her bedroom bell for some hot water. The chambermaid answered that it was ten o'clock, and that there was no fire in the house. Next day, the girl, who was an Irishwoman, had found out that we were Catholics, and exclaimed, 'Sure, if I'd known that, I'd have lighted the fire again, and have boiled the water meeself sooner than that you should have gone without it.' From this time, she was particularly civil and obliging."

After another day's acquaintance, this woman prayed, with tears in her eyes, that we would take her with us. There was a great deal of ill-feeling against her religion, she said, in New York, and she wished to get into a Catholic family. I knew that servants would be more and more scarce the further we went; and as the people of the hotel gave her a good character, my wife consented to her wishes, and I took a place for her to Buffalo.

An American hotel is, in fact, a boarding-house. The highest charge made by any in New York for private bedroom and the use of public sitting-rooms, for tea and breakfast with cold meat, and for dinner of every delicacy, is two-and-a-half dollars per head; the lowest charge is one dollar and a-half. A dollar may be counted as 4*s*. 2*d*. These charges, which include all service except that of porter, are very moderate for a single person: very high when applied to a family of children. Private sitting-rooms and meals in private may, certainly, be had; what may not be had for money? But the innkeepers do not like to be so put out of their way; further west, nothing would induce them so to alter the arrangements of their establishments. Travellers who so exclude themselves in a country whose people live in public, deprive themselves of a great means of becoming acquainted with it. They are disliked; they are thought proud; and are left to themselves. The Battery Hotel is a good second-rate house; both it and the Atlantic are, or were three years ago, the only houses near the sea; all the others—a mile or two up Broadway—are too distant for those who escape from the porters on the quay at half-past ten o'clock at night.

CHAPTER IV.

THE RIVER AND THE RAILROAD.

A sharp man.—The Irish maid.—The river boat.—The Hudson.
—West Point.—The railway *versus* the river.—Selling pets.
—The New World aground.—Albany.—The sharp agency.
—An Albany waiter.—The railway cars.—British delicacy.—
First class trains.—The scenery.—Rome.—Oneida.—Cayuga
Lake.—Geneva.—The burning spring.—Rochester.

I HAD thought myself too old a traveller to be taken in even by a Yankee sharper; but yet I allowed myself to be persuaded, by the people of an office in New York, to take river and railway tickets from them for the whole distance to Buffalo. There are very many of these offices, which profess to forward travellers for much less than the regular fares—pretending either that they have contracted with the different companies, or that they have bought up tickets during a period of competition for less than their present value. Many are the emigrants who are thus induced to contract for their whole passage to the most distant parts of the Union, and who either pay much more than the regular fares, or find their tickets worthless after the first few stages.

I merely mention this to show the state of morality and police in New York. I myself had ascertained what were the regular fares; and lost only some of the contingent advantages promised me by " the Agency" from buying my tickets from them.

The maid, who had besought us to take her with us, had gone home to see her friends, and did not return to the hotel. She knew that we had paid for a place for her for the first five hundred miles, and we thought that we might meet her on the packet. She was not there, and our growing feelings against Irish emigrants in America were not lessened.

On the 5th of June, we walked on board the New World steamer with that facility which my daughter has recorded when we landed at New York: the platform and the deck were so closely and evenly joined that we knew not where one ended and the other began. But what a deck was that of this steamer, which was said to have been recently built and to be the largest in the United

States! Two immense saloons covered half of it, and opened upon a terrace or balcony that ran round them, a few feet above the water. There was, moreover, the open deck in front of the saloon; the deck forward, for second-class passengers and luggage; and the flat roof of the two saloons covered by an awning. I cannot give other dimensions than that the vessel was three hundred and sixty feet long: suffice it to say that the saloons were very large drawing-rooms, receiving light and air from a score or so of windows, opening upon the gallery around, and through which the whole river scenery could be enjoyed by those reclining within. They were fitted up with all the gorgeousness and splendour that could be imparted by gilding, mirrors, chandeliers, rich carpets and couches, and sofas of satin and brocade. Well, indeed, are these steamers called floating palaces! There was one on the river, called the *Rein Deer*, not quite so large as the *New World*, but said to be swifter, and which was even more richly decorated. The only unsightly objects to an English mind were the frequent cut-glass spittoons that bestrewed the carpets, and which I made it a rule to stumble over as I walked up and down.

The main city of New York, exclusive of the suburbs built upon the neighbouring lands, stands upon the point and tongue of land between Long Island Sound and the Hudson river, which comes straight down from the north, and is, therefore, generally spoken of in the country by the name of North River. Up this river, our steamer began to move, at a speed of more than eighteen miles an hour, against current; and passed, in succession, numerous little towns and villages —suburbs of New York and places of holiday resort for its citizens. They were more or less beautifully nestled in the bright scenery on either side;—bright but not striking, till we came to the wonderful precipitous bank of traprock, which rises abruptly from the river, on the western side, to the height of about five hundred feet. These, called the Palissades, are dark and frowning; and extend, an almost impassable boundary, for about twenty miles, as far as Tappan. To our fathers, this was a well known name: General Washington's head-

CHAP. IV.—RIVER AND RAILROAD.

quarters were here, during the war of Independence in 1780, when Major André of the English army was hanged by him as a spy. But Washington Irving's pretty villa soon woos us to pleasanter thoughts, of himself, of Columbus, of Astoria, and of the conquest of Granada: his genius carries our minds away even from this majestic stream, although it here expands into a bay from two to three miles broad. On the top of the rocks, somewhere above here, is a lake four miles in circumference, from which New York is supplied with its best ice; the ice, in winter, is sawed out into large blocks, which are slid down an inclined plane to the river's edge, and kept till the frost breaks up and they can be embarked for the city.

But the shores of the mighty stream contract; high mountains close it in on each side, and in front; there is surely no egress from amongst these frowning rocks? Yes, yes; there is a narrow opening in front, leading direct through the mountains, and there is also one on the right hand, at the base of that towering peak: which will the pilot take? Which of the two ravines shall we explore? Neither. The great steamer almost grazes the base of the naked precipices, and turns sharply round to the left, and threads a chasm down which the waters boil and race. A sinuous channel opens to us amongst the mountains that close behind and on either hand; and, for some miles, we breast a boiling torrent that rushes through magnificent scenery. This is called the Horse Race. Nothing on the Rhine will bear the slightest comparison to it: " it whips all creation."

I have not stopped to describe the state prison at Clinton: no doubt Dickens has fully spoken of it with other institutions of the United States: nor can I now pause amid the lovely scenery of West Point, where Kosciusko loved to meditate, and where the cadets of the military school have erected a handsome monument to his memory. I was informed that this military school is an excellently-conducted institution: unlike our own military academies, according to recent revelations (which I would not believe), the highest sense of honour and honesty exists amongst the pupils;

the slightest falsehood or breach of either is followed by immediate expulsion—insisted on by the other pupils, and gladly acquiesced in by the chiefs. But our steamer takes another sharp turn amid the rocks; the river again expands, and the lovely scenery of Crow's Nest, on its cliff fifteen hundred feet high, engrosses and delights us.

Pass we the thriving town of Poughkeepsie; pass we the village of Catskill, with its distant hills and waterfalls; the train upon the railroad, that runs parallel with the river, is passing them all even quicker than we. Strange that a railway can be maintained in opposition to such splendid water carriage! But, during all the winter, that water carriage is locked up by ice; and then the railway reaps its double harvest. Strange rather that such floating palaces can be maintained, for the summer months only, against a railway that can work during the whole year round! But the steamers communicate with both sides of the river: the railway only with one; and the steamers are, evidently, preferred by all who can convert the transaction of business into a pleasure excursion, through some of the most magnificent scenery in the world. " Several ladies, evidently brides, were now on board the *New World* with us," writes Louie; "and a number of very young mamas, with little squalling babies, whom they alternately scolded and petted. These were confined to the inner saloon, with their nurses. Most of the ladies sat out on the roof-deck, under the awning. When I first went up there, accompanied by mama's little dog, it excited a great deal of admiration amongst all the ladies; for most of the *little* dogs in America are very ugly. Soon after, when my brother, Kenelm, was walking about with it, a man came up to him and said:

" ' How much would you sell me that dog for ?'

" ' I would not sell it at all.'

" ' Well now, I calculate you would not refuse a couple of hundred dollars for it ?'

" ' Indeed I should: it is not to be sold for any money. It is a pet.'

" The man looked very much surprised, and walked away. On another occasion," con-

CHAP. IV.—RIVER AND RAILROAD.

tinues Louie, "a lady asked Lucy for how much she would sell her parrot,—a grey one, and a great rarity there, where they have the green parrots only. Outside the saloon ran a small balcony, on which I stood, with two of my brothers, nearly all the time, looking at the beautiful banks of the Hudson on each side of us. Every now and then, there were breaks in the masses of forest trees, disclosing pretty villas and châlets built of wood."

"Bright and beautiful shone the sun," writes Agnes: "in fact, it was a day to make the beautiful scenery of the Hudson banks appear more beautiful still; and nothing but the scenery could make us stand out under the burning sun that was pouring down upon us. But one does not go on the Hudson every day."

At last, my satirist of America had found something in it to admire!

I was amused to observe the construction of the railroad which, as I have said, runs parallel with the river. It often skirted the waters, and cut across shallows in the bends of the ravines. In these cases, what think you, friend shareholder, the rails rested on? No brick or stone arches; no raised embankment; no piers even for the sleepers to lie upon were there. Wooden piles were driven into the ground, and to these the very sleepers were nailed. The rails lay upon them; and from the deck of the *New World*, I could see the whole fabric shake and tremble as the trains rattled over them, smoking and whistling, and seeming to shout defiance to our steamer.

"Oh my poor shares!" exclaimed an English speculator, to whom I described the engineering of the line.

All the company (not the railway shareholders, but ours of the *New World*) went down to dine. I could not introduce all my children to the *table d'hôte* of these holiday folks; and I bespoke a dinner for us at a separate table. There we eat at our leisure and comfortably; not being obliged to swallow our dinner in ten minutes.

When we went on deck again, the river banks were no longer broken and picturesque, as in the lower half of the Hudson. The hills were more depressed and rounded; the water was sluggish, and often broken up by low muddy islands; the banks were overgrown by reeds; and, at three o'clock, when we had proceeded one hundred and forty miles from New York, and were within sight of Albany, the *New World* ran aground! There was no noise, no objurgation: every one seemed either to have expected the event, or to be used to it, or to be aware that the managers would do the best they could; and the first assurance I had of the fact, was from seeing the passengers pass to the deck of a little steamer that had come alongside of us. In this, we were uncomfortably crowded; but we soon reached Albany. Our luggage was to come up in the *New World*, which would float again when lightened of its passengers. We walked to the hotel; and I went to the agents from whom I had purchased my tickets and booked myself "through" to Buffalo.

I explained to a man whom I found there, that my luggage was on board the steamer, and that I required to have it moved, according to contract, to the hotel for the night, and to be supplied with tickets for Buffalo. He met me civilly, but with much demur; the head clerk was out; and the key of the office could not be found. However, perceiving that I was not to be put off, as, doubtless, hundreds of poor emigrants had been by the same "agency", the head clerk was found, the key of the desk was found; and the requisite number of first-class railway tickets were given in exchange for my New York receipt. The removal of the luggage I could not get them to undertake. They declared that I had more than the proper quantity, and that their New York correspondents could not have intended to charge them with the conveyance of it. Rejoicing that I had, at least, secured my railroad tickets, which they had evidently not intended to give me, I hired other porters, and returned to the hotel.

The fare from New York to Albany by the night boats is one dollar, or fifty cents, or as little as, owing to the usual competition, passengers please to pay; that by the *New World* and *Rein Deer*, the only two day boats, is two dollars and a-half. I was charged sixty cents a head for breakfast on board, and five dollars for our dinner, without wine; and two dollars for extra luggage. But we had passed over a distance of one hundred and forty-five miles.

Albany, so called after the Duke of York and Albany, afterwards James the Second, and one of the oldest towns in the country, is well situated on a rising ground above the river. Its streets are tolerably well built for an old town, and contained about fifty thousand inhabitants. Delavan's Hotel, there, is a large, half-furnished building; it was conducted with the regularity of a military boarding house, but without refinement or consideration for the comfort of its customers; it was a sort of caravanserai, where men walked in or out, and smoked about the passages and corridors, at their pleasure; the only regulation being that they should take their meals at beat of gong, or not at all, and pay the established price for their board. The ladies' sitting-room here, also, was large and handsomely furnished: the bed-rooms were very plain.

"Next morning," writes Louie, "we were

sitting at breakfast and our parents had not yet made their appearance, when a waiter came up to Kenelm, who hated everything that he thought savoured of 'liberty and equality,' and said to him, 'Is the old man down yet?'

"'What old man?'

"'Why, *the* old man, to be sure.'

"'I do not know who you mean.'

"'Why the old man, your father, of course.'

"My brother, very angry, said, 'I am not accustomed to hear my father spoken of in such a manner.'

"The waiter stared and went away laughing."

When "the old man," that's I, came in afterwards, I found the table loaded with tea and coffee, with hot rolls and hot corn bread, with sweetmeats, molasses, pancakes, and lots of cold meat: it was more like a north country than an English or European breakfast. Negro waiters were in attendance, much to the surprise and dislike of my younger children, who complained of their dirty hands. I myself was very favourably impressed by their quiet way of moving about, and by their civil attentions. It was not a negro, but an Irish waiter, who had given me brevet rank as " the old man."

Albany is 145 miles from New York, 200 from Boston, 250 from Montreal, and 325 from Buffalo : in America, it is considered to be a most central situation. In Europe, it would be thought quite out of reach of any of these its neighbouring towns !

I was surprised to find the railway carriages drawn up upon a tram-road a few steps from our hotel, in a street in the centre of Albany. No fence of any kind parted it from the crowded thoroughfare. We took our places and the train dashed onwards through the crowd. An English railway carriage is generally divided into three compartments, or three double-bodied coaches, with three or four seats in each, half of which look towards the engine and half from it ;—the knees of the occupants meeting in the passage between : in England, each compartment is entered by a door in the two sides which shut in this passage : and the several carriages, of three compartments each, are hooked on to one another—no communication being possible between them. We had entered the car, on which we were now travelling, at the end: a passage led down the centre from end to end: on each side of this passage, were sofas of cut velvet large enough to hold two persons comfortably. The backs of the sofas were moveable on hinges, so that a party of four could sit facing each other, or they could always be moved to face or turn from the engine. At the end of each sofa, was a window in the side of the carriage, with glass, and venetian blind or curtain. Here, therefore, was no quartering of legs, since all sat the same way; no pushing past knees, as the passage in the centre gave ample space to move up and down, and the seat on each side held only two persons, who had a window between them. But there was also a door at each end of the passage leading in and out of the carriage to the ground by a double flight of steps; and with a little landing place, or platform as they called it, which touched a similar platform at the end of the next carriage, and so afforded the means of stepping from one to the

CHAP. IV.—RIVER AND RAILROAD. 109

other and of passing entirely from one to the other end of the train. People were requested not to stand on this platform, as those who did so encumbered the way and might be thrown down by a jolt or sudden stoppage: but the space was generally occupied by some who stood there to smoke, notwithstanding the prohibition.

We had not proceeded far when I observed the guard, as we should call him in Europe, though here he was distinguished by no dress or badge of office, moving from end to end of the train, and taking the fare and giving tickets to those who had not had time or inclination to take them before. Here was a saving of time: and the man would sit down by the side of any passenger for a chat, or to give information required. We had not proceeded far when I observed boys walking from end to end of the train, offering iced water to those who wished for it; others had time-tables of the different railways or steamers that we should come across, and cards of the hotels which they were engaged to recommend in the different towns. One passenger came up to another near me and seated himself beside him, while I heard him say that he had sought his friend through the whole line of cars, as they are called, before he found him here. This power of locomotion had evidently its advantages. I, too, got up to study the contrivances about me; and passed from one carriage to the other. In the corner of one of them an oblong space was partitioned off: I opened the door into it and found myself in a little room neatly fitted up with chairs, washhand bason and ewer, and—a watercloset. This, indeed, was a pleasing discovery; as it removed one great difficulty, which the father of eleven children could not but have foreseen, in this journey of three hundred and twenty-five miles for which we had booked ourselves. On the English York and London and other lines, when the train stopped for a quarter of an hour for refreshment, I had observed a hundred and fifty women all first rushing, after five hours' confinement, to the little space set apart for them, and which might accommodate half a dozen at a time: I had seen the anxious glances of those who were unable to gain admission there while they were fainting for the food which they had deferred taking: I had seen their look of suffering as the bell rang while they were still detained outside the door; and I had heard some expostulate angrily with the guard and dare him to move the train, while they and the many around them were excluded from the still closed door and overcrowded precincts:—they would start again without refreshment, but the other, they said, they would not forego! And this is English delicacy! And I shall be reproached for describing on paper what every man who travels on an English railway witnesses with his own eyes; what every woman suffers from and blushes for. Faugh!

Each of the cars I now inspected contained from ten to twenty seats on each side of the passage; giving, therefore, accommodation to from forty to eighty travellers. Not half of the places were engaged. The occupants were of every class above that of labourers; for a division of classes in a railway train, would be incompatible with American feelings: they have, indeed, express trains and mail trains, but the fares on all are the same: and their only way of enabling the poorer citizens to avail themselves of railroads without shocking their own and the public sense of decorous equality, has been by the invention of what they call "emigrant trains". These are cheaper and slower, and perform, for example, in twenty-six hours the three hundred and twenty-eight miles which we, in the express train, were now doing in ten hours. Emigrants do not pretend, as yet, to an equality with other citizens; and public feeling does not think them insulted by having a cheaper, a distinct train provided for them. If citizens please to avail themselves of it, that is their own affair: they are supposed to do so for their own convenience, not as acknowledging any inferiority!

And yet, from the motley assemblage we met in these railway cars, we never experienced the slightest annoyance. When there was other space, no one intruded into a sofa which had already one occupant. Americans are cleaner in their linen and clothes than Europeans; and though their sentiments of independence and common citizenship, give them a manner and tone of equality, yet they also give them a sentiment of self-respect which prevents them doing what would lower them in public opinion. During all this day's journey, I saw, besides the person who collected fares and tickets in the carriages, no railway official in apparent authority, no policeman : — every American seems to consider himself interested in the preservation of order. A moral Lynch law governs the intercourse of all: for all being, more or less, dependent upon the public opinion of all, no class can afford to despise the public opinion of another class. As one proof of this general sentiment, I record that a rope passes from each car communicating with a bell beside the driver, so that any passenger may ring it in case of illness or accident. When such a contrivance has been suggested for English railway carriages, the objection has always been that the train would be constantly stopped by the whim or the malice of silly or mischievous travellers.

But, meanwhile, our cars are rattling forwards, with no great motion, and at a fair pace; for although our average speed for the three hundred and twenty-eight miles does not exceed twenty-eight miles an hour, yet that speed, when moving, is, in reality, much greater, because our train makes so many stoppages to take in passengers and for refreshment. Leaving the glorious Hudson River at Albany, we had soon crossed over to the banks of the romantic Mohawk; and, for miles, the railway and the great Erie canal followed all its windings amid those picturesque pine-covered rocks. The inhabited country might be a mere track through a desert: but yet the track was all alive. Railroad, canal, aqueducts, saw-mills, and smiling villages, connected together by log-houses and châlets, gave the whole a look of perhaps greater animation, than can be found in many an old settled country; as a spot of ground, in which bricklayers and carpenters are building a house, swarms with activity much more than the same space when the quietly inhabited house is secluded in its own flower garden. About Little Falls, a rising village of some three thousand souls, the scenery is quite Swiss: homely Swiss scenery without the Alps.

Indeed, the whole of this line on the banks of the Mohawk river, for about one hundred miles, would be considered beautiful or very pleasing in any country. What, then, must it have seemed to us to whom everything around had the additional charm of novelty!

We passed through Frankfort, through Utica; we passed through Rome even; and thought its streets and squares so wide, and laid out and rising with so much regularity, as to shame its crumbling historic prototype; we passed Oneida, with a classical sound of its own, far dearer, to the European traveller in America, than any sham reminiscence of ancient Europe; and we came on to Syracuse. The train dashed, as usual, into the middle of the town, and stopped there. Waiters, in front of half-a-dozen hotels, were ringing their dinner bells in the crowded street; we went into that which we deemed most inviting, and found an excellent dinner, which we were allowed ample time to eat, and for which I was charged four dollars and twenty-five cents, or about eighteen pence a head.

At Syracuse, another canal and railroad

branched off to Oswego, on Lake Ontario; we followed our line due west, past the beautiful village of Auburn, on Lake Owasco, and over the sunny bosom of the Cayuga Lake. I say over it, for the railroad here cut across the northern end of it, on a bridge about a mile and a quarter long, and gave us a view of scenery which reminded me strongly of that of the Lake of Garda, but was far more beautiful. The water was strangely transparent; and when we passed, it slept waveless amid its smiling, well-cultivated shores, and reflected a sun as bright as any in Italy. This lake is about forty miles long, and from one to four miles broad, and is so deep, that it never freezes even in the coldest winters. It would be difficult to find anywhere a country more beautiful, more pleasingly attractive, than the shores of these five lakes of Skaneteles, Owasco, Cayuga, Seneca, and Canandaigua; lovely sheets of water, all of them lying parallel to one another on the northern ridge of the high ground between the ocean and the great lakes, where it slopes down towards Lake Ontario. We looked at all these charming valleys and gently sloping hills, and fancied a home for our sons amongst them; but I had determined to choose a warmer climate than this is in the winter, and to go into one of the western states, where the best of the land should not be already bought up. Still, the prospect of founding a home amid similar scenery, gave it an additional interest in our eyes.

Leaving, therefore, Lake Ontario on our right hand, we passed, in succession, the northern extremities of these five beautiful pieces of water, dotted with steamers and other boats, and hastened through the flourishing villages on their banks. At the outlet of each, towards Ontario, is a water-power, of which the greatest use is made; grist mills, and saw mills, and tanneries evince the mechanical industry of the inhabitants. We passed through Waterloo, and enjoyed some refreshing lemonade at Geneva; I record these names from their amusing absurdity. Why will not Americans have a country of their own, instead of trying to pass it off as a bastard Europe? On, past the beautiful lake of Seneca, we sped to the still more charming neighbourhood of Canandaigua Lake ; whose deep clear waters, never frozen over, though lying amid high grounds, teem with fish. In this neighbourhood, is one of those natural phenomena, so frequent in America, called the Burning spring ; gas bubbles up through the water of a small stream, or through the snow that covers it in winter ; and, when a light has been applied, burns steadily down to the snow or the water's edge. In very cold weather, tubes of ice are formed round the several jets of gas, which, if then lighted, seems to have been conducted by art into these beautiful ice-crystal candelabras.

The whole of New York state abounds with mineral springs, which are more or less resorted to. Many of them are said to arise in most romantic scenery.

We passed through Rochester, a town, in 1850, of thirty-seven thousand inhabitants; as it had then doubled its population in the preceding ten years, it is impossible to say what it may be now. It is built on the Genessee river ; and owes its prosperity to the immense

CHAP. IV.—RIVER AND RAILROAD. 119

water-power which thus enables it to manufacture daily five thousand of those barrels of flour which, thence conveyed by Lake Ontario and the Saint Lawrence, are introduced into England free of duty; a manufactured article with which our corn growers and our millers have to compete. Import the unground grain, if ye will, duty free; but flour is no longer a raw material, and should be subject to the same duties as are paid by other manufactured goods. Railroads and canals on every side extend the commerce and the prosperity of Rochester.

We did not pause to visit the famous Genessee Falls; but kept our places in our cars, and arrived at half-past seven o'clock at Buffalo; tired, indeed, but delighted with this our first incursion into the mainland of America.

CHAPTER V.

NIAGARA FALLS.

The " gals."—Buffalo.—The churches.—St. Patrick's church.
The lapdog.—The railway accident.—The runaway slave.—
Roasting and shooting niggers.—Niagara falls.—Goat or
Iris island.—The Horseshoe Fall.—Fishing.—The tower.—
The American Falls.—Mr. Geo. W. Sims and the ferry.—
Canadian and American manners.—The lost hat.—Canadian
and American prosperity.

" Buffalo gals ! can't ye come out to-night,
Can't ye come out to-night, can't ye come out to-night ?
Buffalo gals ! can't ye come out to night,
And dance by de light of de moon !"

How little I thought, only a few months ago, when I used to sing these unmeaning words to their beautiful air, that I should ever visit the distant Indian village to which they referred : —a distant Indian village, I imagined it, somewhere in the backwoods, but I did not know where ; and I pictured it to myself composed of wigwams, built of wood, and overshadowed by eternal forests beside one of those great inland seas of America which Europeans scarcely know by name! Such were my musings as, passing from the crowded wharves and canals of Lower Buffalo, I sauntered up a handsome street, one hundred and twenty feet broad and two miles long, and, thence, to the more retired streets and squares on the higher ground. Here I overlooked the broad Lake of Erie at my feet; the green hills of Canada before me; and, at the distance of a few miles on my right hand, the far-stretching expanse of Lake Ontario. It was a beautiful morning; the sun shone brightly athwart the clouds that, ever and anon, sent down slight showers to wet and refreshen the air. The raindrops danced and glistened on the laburnum and acacia blossoms and the trellised roses that peeped over the garden walls that enclosed a little space in front of almost every house. We had staid here to rest on the preceding day; and, on this, Whit-Sunday, we were seeking out a place of Catholic worship.

And here, I first observed the systematic grouping of churches which seems to obtain almost everywhere in the United States. You may pass a village, perhaps, though rarely, that

that has no church at all; but if it has one, it will certainly have four. In the towns, churches stand in groups of four, as near together as possible. It is the spirit of competition. As one lawyer in a village always makes work for two, so does one sectarian preacher provoke a religious feeling which others are required to satisfy with opposing doctrines.

The Catholic churches do not appear to form part of these groups. I discovered that Buffalo was the seat of a bishop, and contained four English and Irish, one French and two German Catholic churches. I made my way to St. Patrick's—then the largest church, though a magnificent cathedral was being raised near it. The building was crowded — almost to suffocation. The congregation appeared very respectable:—all were very clean and well-dressed. Yet I was told that almost all were Irish emigrants escaped from starvation and forced idleness at home. I lingered about the door, as the congregation went in and came out; yet, amongst three thousands of Irish, not one asked for alms!

The preacher's Irish accent declared his origin, although he had been in the United States long enough to acquire American phraseology: for example; while recommending good will and amity amongst nations, he told them not to imitate " Balaak *canvassing* Balaam to curse the Israelites". The word " canvassing", in such a sense, must have been picked up on this side of the Atlantic! Then, referring to the festival of the day, the preacher gave us a very tolerable burst of declamation on the universality and uniformity of his faith: assuring the poor wanderers from a distant land that, as they had found the same religion at Buffalo, so, " far as the winds blow or the waters roll, it is to be found the same everywhere as here."

The number of our pets was lessening. Another of our canary birds died at Buffalo. Our poor little dog had been ailing during the greater part of the voyage out; and though it had seemed to recover at times, so as to excite the admiration of many who again stopped us here offering to buy it (which seems, in this country, to be thought a delicate, complimentary way of expressing admiration), it now grew much worse and died in the course of this night. My wife and children happily foresaw not the greater trials they were to undergo; and were much afflicted by this loss of another of their pets. A lap-dog had died in my family at Florence twenty years before; and its mistress, an elderly lady who sat up with it, had declared that, the instant her dog expired, the night lamp had suddenly gone out! Carlo was buried in the garden of the Hôtel Fetherstonhaugh at Florence: little I then thought that, twenty years later, I should see another pet lap-dog taken from my apartment and buried in the garden of the Exchange Hotel at Buffalo!

This was a tolerable inn close to the railway station (which had been its recommendation to me), or close, rather, to the point where the Rochester Railway runs into the town. We witnessed a sad consequence of the unenclosed, unguarded state of these precincts:— a little boy had been playing and clambering about on one of the cars, when it was put in motion. He fell, and the wheels went over both his thighs. The poor child was carried to our hotel, and laid in a lower room: a surgeon attended, and much sympathy seemed to be felt for him. But it was evidently impossible to save his life; and he died on the following day. His poor mother was in a state of distress that may be imagined:—a distress aggravated by the refusal of the surgeon to permit her to see her child, lest the interview should agitate him. Cruel caution to both!

The mother was standing outside the door; while one of my sons, who was passing the open window, heard the little sufferer cry, " Mother! mother! why don't you come to me?"

" She will come to-morrow", some one said soothingly; " but it would make you worse if she came to night."

" I don't care if I am worse", he cried; " for if I die, I shall go to heaven. But I want to see mother!"

Cruel caution, indeed; which, under no circumstance, could avail to save life; and the propriety of which would be very doubtful, even if it were certain to have the desired effect. Woe to those who thrust themselves between relatives on their death-bed! Woe to those who conceal their condition from the dying, whatever may be the danger of revealing it!

A great deal of excitement existed at this time in Buffalo, not only amongst what is called " the coloured population", but also amongst the " whites"; and, from Buffalo, extended through the length and breadth of the United States. New York is a free state—that is to say, it permits not its citizens to possess slaves within its boundaries; nor could any fugitive slave be pursued and recovered in it until a general law, passed in the preceding year, authorised slave owners from slave states, not only to follow and seize their runaways in the territory of free states, but, also, compelled all private citizens and authorities in free states to assist in capturing and reconducting them to their owners when called upon to do so. A fugitive slave, in fact, was looked upon in the same light as a thief who had run away with his master's property, and all the confederation of friendly states constituting the Union, were called upon to aid in arresting the robber. It was in vain that citizens of free states declared that slavery was as repugnant to them as to the feelings of Englishmen, and protested against being made to do violence to those feelings by aiding in re-enslaving a fellow creature who had fled amongst them for protection. They were reminded that, by the very first principles of the federative union, every state was independent as to its own internal legislation, and that the rules of goodfellowship required that each should assist the other in carrying out that legislation, and in the restoration of "lost, strayed, or stolen" property. I myself could not quite see how one position necessarily followed from the other: obligations exist, by treaty, between England and the United States, but England does not therefore surrender all slaves who may have escaped to Canada. However, I confine myself now to facts, and return to the cause of the excitement at Buffalo.

A man named Rust had been just sent there by Mr. George H. Moore of Louisville, Kentucky, in search of a slave named Daniels, whom the said Mr. Moore claimed as his property. Rust, having found out that Daniels was living as cook on board one of the Erie steam-boats, went on deck and had him called up from below. Daniels, suspecting no harm, was ascending the ladder to come on deck, when Rust caught up a billet of wood that lay ready for the furnace, struck him with it on the back of his head just as it emerged from below, and knocked him down the ladder. He fell upon the hot stove in the cook's room, where he lay senseless, bleeding and burning, until he was taken off, " badly fried, and with the blood running from his nose, mouth and ears." Thus helpless and stupified, he was carried before Mr. Commissioner Henry K. Smith, before whom it was proved, even by the witnesses for the claimant, that Daniels had been repeatedly sent by said claimant on his own business into the free state of Ohio, and that he had come away from Ohio, and not from Kentucky, to Buffalo; so that, it was asserted, he could not be said to have escaped from a slave state. It was declared that this interpretation of the wording of the law had been sanctioned by the highest tribunals. Mr. Commissioner Smith, however, chose to read it differently, and decided against the black. But his owner had no predilection for Daniels: he only wished for the value of his property: and when lawyer Talcroft, on the part of the claimant, suggested that the condemned slave should be sent to prison while a telegraphic message was forwarded to Kentucky to inquire at what price Mr. Moore would sell him, in case white sympathisers and free blacks in Buffalo should be able and willing to ransom him, and when he had advised free negroes in the court to go quietly home and wait for the reply, Mr. Commissioner Smith had backed the advice in these words:

" And I also have a few words to say to the coloured people here. If there is no telegraph sent at all, that slave shall go back to his master, according to my decision; and if you dare to oppose that decision by force, *you will be* SHOT DOWN."

It may readily be supposed that great irritation and excitement prevailed at Buffalo amongst all classes while this was going on. Another magistrate was appealed to, and the slave-catcher, Rust, was bound over for trial, in the sum of one thousand dollars, to answer a charge of assault and battery, for having stricken down the slave with a piece of wood. Daniels, however, still lay in jail.

On Monday morning, we started in railway cars, from the centre of one of the busiest streets in the town, to go to Niagara Falls, distant twenty-two miles. The road skirts the shore of Niagara river, which here is about three miles broad, winding slowly on through unpicturesque scenery, and amongst several uninteresting islands. Be it remembered, that this river is the outlet towards the sea of all the waters of Lake Erie, Lake Huron, Lake Michigan, and Lake Superior, which cover about one hundred and fifty thousand square miles, and are supposed to contain nearly one half of the fresh water on the surface of the globe. Lazily it went along, between its low and rather marshy banks. We neared Niagara.

Boys and waiters passed through the cars recommending different hotels; for Niagara Falls is a holiday place for the Buffaloes, as, I presume, the inhabitants of the city call themselves: handbills, like those which Messrs.

CHAP. V.—NIAGARA FALLS.   131

Moses throw into London omnibusses and cabs, came flying in at the windows. I copy one of them :—

FERRY AT THE FALLS!

This ferry, immediately at the foot of the GREAT CATARACT, where the spectator has in crossing, the whole scene of falling water before him in all its majesty and power, is in its accustomed order for the accommodation of the public.

The Ferry is provided with spacious open barges, which carry with entire safety 20 to 30 passengers each, and the crossing is accomplished in about five minutes. The landing place is reached by a flight of covered stairs, 290 in number, down the bank, or by a parallel inclined plane, 360 feet long, on which Cars are moved by stationary Water Power.

Visitors wishing to reach the Falls most expeditiously and economically, should at once, on the arrival of the morning Train from Buffalo, at half-past ten, proceed directly down the street in which the Cars stop, *passing by the Buffalo Depot*, through the Grove to the Ferry, distant less than a five minutes walk. Not a moment should be lost, for the sun soon attains an elevation which deprives the scene of one of its most

STRIKING BEAUTIES,

THE

MORNING RAINBOW.

In fifteen or twenty minutes, they stand on the famed

TABLE ROCK, ON THE BRITISH SHORE.

One hour will suffice to make the whole trip, crossing and returning, and allow the visitor an half hour on the Table. Indeed he may pass nearly an hour there and be back at his hotel, on this side, by noon. Or, if he prefers, he may take a Carriage from Table Rock, directly to the Suspension Bridge, after passing which to the American shore, he can return to the Village by a like conveyance.

Fare to Canada, including the use of the descending Car or Steps, as may be preferred, 18 3-4 cents. Freight and Baggage passed with perfect facility, at low rates.

The safety of this Ferry is best appreciated from the fact that it has been in use more than 40 years—formerly with very light boats, and even small canoes, and that not a human life has been lost in passing it. On reaching the Canada shore, the bank is there ascended by a free wagon road, at the foot of which Carriages are always in waiting.

The subscriber having passed his whole life at this place, is prepared and will be happy to impart any local information that may be desired.

GEO. W. SIMS.
At the Ferry, American Shore.

☞ P.S.—The use of the great Staircase and grounds adjacent is free to Visitors.

NIAGARA FALLS, 1851.

It will be observed that, according to George W. Sims, the Ferry is the object most worth visiting at Niagara. So did others particularly recommend other localities, in which they themselves were interested. We descended from the cars, disregarding them all. Disregarding, also, the many who offered themselves as guides, we crossed the street, and followed the press of other passengers who, we thought, must be like us, visitors to the world-wonder. They fell off into the hotels, to the right and to the left; thus showing that they were only holiday people from Buffalo. We pursued our solitary way towards the river. Now, here, although we were but about a quarter of a mile from the cascade, I cannot say that we heard those sounds like distant thunder which deafen many travellers to Niagara, almost from the time they have left Albany. At the end of the street, we saw trees, and a rush of water. Amongst stones and rocks, and little islands, through which two or three solitary firs struck their naked roots into the stones beneath, they rushed; foaming and boiling, and splashing, and eddying. A rustic bridge spanned them, resting upon piers of jagged stone. We stood on the centre of it, and I asked my children what they thought of Niagara.

They were disappointed. These were very beautiful; but they thought there was a cataract.

These were the Rapids on the American side. Listen now to the dull booming sound a-head! . . . . . .

At the end of the bridge, on a little island

called Bath Island, we were called upon to pay a toll, twenty-five cents for each person:—for one visit? This would free us for the whole season; and the toll-taker said we could not tell how often we might return to it. Was it prophecy or experience that inspired him?....

With other twenty-five cents, I bought from him a guide book with a map; and so, independent of chattering guides which this toll happily kept back, we crossed over another smaller bridge, and stood upon Goat Island; since denominated by these gentry, in the hope of making Niagara more attractive, Iris Island.

Delightful were the natural paths amongst the brambles and underwood, or on the green grass shaded by lofty oak trees, the immemorial forest of Goat Island! Our children were overjoyed with the wild gooseberries they picked, and with the fresh natural feeling of this their first country walk since they had left Talence to embark on the *Kate Hunter.* We pursued our walk to the right, and, skirting the southern side of the island, saw down below us, and athwart the overhanging boughs, the

CHAP. V.—NIAGARA FALLS. 135

American Rapids still boiling onwards, onwards in their headlong career.

A path struck off to the left, from whence the sound came louder and louder. We turned into it and soon emerged on the other side of the island.

The Great Horseshoe Fall was close before us.

Nearer—nearer came the waters.

Majestic, in the majesty with which they had recovered themselves after the hurrying and chafing of the rapids on this the Canadian side, on—on they come; a peaceful, though rapid, river. The channel is here about half-a-mile broad; and onwards—onwards come the overflow of half the fresh waters on the globe. A rapid and peaceful river, on they come. Suddenly the earth, the solid rock-bed, fails beneath them. They spring forwards unsupported. The sun glances through them; and they gleam with hues more than any emerald bright. For a moment, they gleam; and then, down—down—down they go. A cauldron of froth and spray receives them. Clouds of white foam uprise from the rock-girt pit below, and hide whither they are gone, and what has become of them. But there again—lower down still—one hundred and sixty feet below the ledge from which they had sprung, there again they emerge from the foam-clouds; dark blue, almost angry black, though breaking occasionally into short, curling, flashing waves—on they go indignant, on they hurry, they roll, they race from the scene of their discomfiture. They dig themselves a channel three hundred feet deep below their own surface; and onwards, in that wild but narrow ravine, between those close overhanging rocks, onwards they hurry, they roll, they race from the scene of their discomfiture.

But is it all over? No: not so. Look above. There where ye marked them first come on majestically slow; there where the rock-bed, cut away in the centre in the shape of a segment of a circle, or of a horse-shoe, fails beneath them; there where transparent, emerald-green, they leapt from the precipice and fell down—down into the foam-cauldron below; there onwards, onwards still they come in their majesty; there they leap: there they fall. A sentiment of infinitude, of eternity, oppresses the mind. Onwards they ever come; down, down they ever fall. So have they done since the world was made ; so will they continue to do while the world endures.

" The voice of the Lord is upon the waters: the God of majesty speaketh in the thunder : the earth trembled and shook : the Lord ruleth the floods : the Lord is king for ever."

Steps, called Biddler's stairs, lead down from Goat Island to the foot of the cascade, where the water first emerges from its seething foam-cauldron. Here is said to be one of the finest fishing places in the world. I can well believe it. What great fish, that could come and tumble about in such a scene: diving down three hundred feet among the blue waters, or leaping up into the foam-cloud : battling in the current, and triumphing over the broken waters,—what great fish, that could come here, would mope, sleepily, in any other pool ? But it must be a big fish to enjoy this turmoil! What fins, what a tail he must have to divide and lash the whirling waves!

In the water, at some distance from the land, above the cascade, just at the edge of the rock before it breaks away under the river bed, a tower is built nearly fifty feet high. A rude bridge, resting upon not very steady natural piers of rock, leads to it from the island. We felt nervous as our children crossed it: for we were all aware, that, should any one stumble on the rude planking, or fall through the open rails, nothing could save him from being hurried into the gulf below. We went to the top of the tower by a flight of easy steps, and there found an open balustrade, from which we looked, in security, on the magnificent uproar beneath us. The spray flew up from below even to where we were, more than two hundred feet above the bottom of the fall; and double, aye triple, rainbows danced upon its curling eddies.

We returned to Goat Island, rejoicing that the so-called Terrapin Bridge, which used to spring out from the rocks at the base of the tower, and project some ten feet over the edge of the Horseshoe Fall, had been recently washed away; so that our nerves were not tried in having to pass to the end of it.

We turned to the left, and skirted the

northern side of Goat Island, below the Canadian or Horseshoe Fall. Again we were overshadowed by lofty oak trees, as we circled round its eastern extremity. They opened: and the American Falls swept down before us. Never was a more beautiful prospect! The branch of the river on the American side of Goat Island is not so wide; the mass of waters is not so great; but the scenery is more broken—more wooded; the height, even, of the cascade is greater. Down, down they tumbled amid the overhanging boughs, and were received into clouds of their own foam at the bottom. Then, immediately mingling with the Canadian branch of the river that had come down the great Horseshoe Fall, they swept on their way together, and sped adown the narrow ravine towards Lake Ontario. I have seen the Falls of Tivoli, of Terni, of Schaffhausen: were there no Horseshoe Fall, the American Falls of Niagara would be incomparably the grandest—as they are, even now, incomparably the most beautiful—in the world.

We could not linger. It was hopeless to

try to look one's fill. We retraced our steps: passed again over Bath Island and its bridge; across the noisy American rapids; and prepared to follow the advice of Mr. Geo. W. Sims. His " descending car or steps" are at no great distance. Our children were tired and would not explore farther. My wife and I seated ourselves on a wooden sofa, and were let down an inclined plane to the water edge. There we found a boat capable of holding about ten people, and a young fellow, perhaps Mr. Geo. W. Sims himself, beside it. I had seldom seen a more doggedly-impudent-looking countenance. We seated ourselves in the boat; but there he stood, silent and heedless. Why did he not put off? We had not paid our fare, seventy-three cents across and back. Could we not pay it in the boat? No; he would not touch an oar till all was paid. Pocketing the money, he leisurely seated himself and pulled out into the torrent. His handbill said that it was a five minutes' passage: it took us double that time to cross; and indeed good nerves were required to sit unmoved in that cockleshell, tossing upon the angry eddies as they rushed, at storm-pace, beneath us.

We landed on the Canadian shore. Here two or three fly-men touched their hats and offered their vehicles to take us to Table Rock. They said their fare to go there and return was half a dollar. I asked the one I selected if he would have it before he mounted the coachbox: he shook his head smiling, and shrugged his shoulders as he looked to the American. I must own that the behaviour of the two races thus separated by a short ferry, contrasted unfavourably for the citizen. Not that citizens are necessarily brutes; but, in Europe, a ferryman who should behave like one, would be turned adrift by his employer.

A quarter of an hour's drive brought us up the steep bank of the river, past a good-looking hotel, to the edge of the far-famed Table Rock. This is merely a ledge which stands out, somewhat further than the others, over the chasm in front of the Horseshoe Fall. In itself, it is a mere platform: but the view from it is everlasting grand! I use the words advisedly; as it has been, so it will be for everlasting. It is more directly in front of the fall than we had been on Goat Island, and from it all the width and depth is more fully seen. Let it, however, be understood that here are no accessories of scenery; perhaps the fall itself is grander without them: but let it be understood that the great Canadian branch of the river comes on towards the cascades between naked unbroken banks on a level with its surface; and that no trees fringe its current, no broken rocks diversify its banks. Unadorned, in its native grandeur, it comes along: unadorned, in its native grandeur it springs into the chasm.

We declined the offer to descend the stairs from the Table Rock, and to proceed, on a slippery ledge, behind the cascade, as it arches over in its fall; although Appleton's excellent guide-book did assure us that "a gentleman" had charge of it and furnished dresses to prevent the adventurous from being too much wetted by the spray. We returned in our carriage to the gentleman at the ferry-boat, Mr. George W. Sims. Two other passengers were in it already, and he pulled from the bank. From this ferry is, perhaps, the grandest view of all; for the boat passes close in front of both the American and the Horseshoe Falls, and you are enabled to take in as much of both at once as their magnitude will allow. It was a magnificent sight; and we were almost forgetting our apparently dangerous position, when a little steamer rushed beside us to the foot of the cascades and buried itself in their mist. Our ferryman pulled on one side, and his straw hat was blown from his head upon the rushing water. He turned round his ferry-boat and prepared to follow it.

"Surely," I exclaimed, " you are not going to attempt to recover your hat out of this boiling surge!"

" I guess you won't hinder me," he sulkily replied, as he plied his oars, and whirled the canoe hither and thither across and down the hurrying torrent. No danger, perhaps; perhaps nothing to terrify those who were daily accustomed to the ferry; but certainly a kind of boat race or rather hat race, which no one who sees that river for the first time would adventure upon for the value of the said hat, were it full of solid gold. It was recovered, however; the *Maid of the Mist* steamer again swept past us; a band was playing on its deck; and we landed at the old place, and were drawn up the inclined plane. Here I paid twenty-five cents for our slide up and down, and told the "gentleman" who took the toll what I thought of Mr. George W. Sims.

The cars were drawn up in the centre of Fall Street; the holiday folks were hastening to them from the several hotels; we also took our places and returned to Buffalo, wondering whether I should ever again see this world wonder; but quite certain that the toll, two dollars, I had paid for the family run of Goat Island during the remainder of this season could, under no circumstances, avail us again.

In the cars, I studied the map prefixed to the guide book I had purchased. On one side of Niagara river, it showed truly enough, the plan of a considerable village which I knew, from the bustle about several apparently first-rate hotels, really to exist, and to exist in great activity—two railroads starting from it.

On the other side of the river, on the Canadian side, it showed four dots inscribed "Clifton house", "Camera obscura", "Museum", "Table rock"; these also, I knew to exist, for I had passed them; but it likewise gave, as far as the paper would allow, a " Plan of proposed City of the Falls", intersected by a railroad, the whole of which I knew to be imaginary. Yet, why is this? Why do we find a flourishing town and community on one side, and a desert on the other? Let it not be said that it is because the land on the one side is part of the United States, and on the other is subject to England. Let not this be said. But what answer can we make to those who will say so? What answer can we make to those who tell us that this very town of Buffalo had been a small military post, and was burnt to the ground by English and Indians forty years ago; that, twenty-five years ago, it contained only twenty-five hundred inhabitants; and that its population is now upwards of forty thousand: what can we answer to those who give us these statistics, and ask for something corresponding from the Canadian side?

CHAPTER VI.

LAKE ERIE.

The Mayor of Buffalo and the porters.—The night of a nurse.—Lake Erie.—Cross questions and crooked answers.—Emigration.—Sandusky City.—Labels for railway luggage.—Through the forest.—Log houses and frame houses.—A worm fence.—Clearings.—Agriculture of Ohio.—Arrival at Cincinnati.

RETURNING from Niagara Falls, we had tea with our five youngest children, whom we had left at the hotel at Buffalo, and then drove to the quay and embarked on the *Empire* steamer on Lake Erie. The porter brought our baggage on board; I gave it in charge to the steward, who was to pay particular attention to it for a particular remuneration. The hotel porter then made some extraordinary charge for himself, the nature of which I now forget; but which I positively refused to pay. Hereupon occurred a scene such as we read of in old novels. The porter threatened to take back my luggage in lieu of payment; and I warned the steward that, the luggage being committed to his charge, I should hold the steamer responsible if any of it was touched. The porter would call a sheriff's officer. I told him to do so. I watched him go across the quay, and presently return with a companion.

" I am an officer," said he, " sent to enforce payment of this gentleman's charge (N.B. the " gentleman" was the porter.)

" What is his charge?" I asked.

This was a puzzler; and the confederate appealed to his principal; being informed thereon, he returned to me.

" What is your own name?" I asked.

His name, he said, mattered not. He came from the mayor of Buffalo.

" And the mayor of Buffalo has given judgment on the statement of your friend only! Show me the judgment, and your authority."

The confederate was staggered, and both began to bully.

" Hark ye, gentlemen," said I; " the mayor of Buffalo has just gone on board the steamer. Look! there he is on deck—that tall gentleman with his lady and child. Let us go and appeal to him."

The two confederates looked in the direction in which I pointed; then looked at one another; and then, turning on their heels, quickly disappeared.

I went up to the mayor of Buffalo and told him what had just occurred. He was much amused; and expressed regret that he had not become acquainted with his self-constituted officer. He was a pleasant, well-informed man, and was going on a little trip westward with his family.

As our voyage was to last through the night, it was necessary to select cabins. I found on board the steamer, two or three separate rooms on deck with full sized beds in them; and for a small additional charge, I secured one of these for myself and my wife. They called them Bride's rooms. The eleven children of the "bride" were not so comfortably bestowed. In order to show the uninitiated how nurses often spend the night, I copy an extract from the journal of Lucy, my late invalid of Talence, but whom the sea voyage had completely restored to health : " The steamer", she writes, " was built on much the same plan as the *New World* ; but, instead of the separate inner nursery, there was one public ladies' saloon, with berths round it, in which all we girls had the pleasure of sleeping. No strangers were there, except a neat little Irishwoman and her baby ; another very quiet respectable-looking old lady ; and an old woman who had never been on the water before, and had expressed her fears to me throughout the evening, exclaiming, ' Now I hope there won't be a storm !' ' Ain't you afeard the biler'l bust, and that if it did, we should all be lost.' The novelty of my situation, in the upper berth over my sister, and the light in the cabin kept me awake : but I was just beginning to doze at about one o'clock, when the door of the ladies' washing-room opened and my friend, the timid old woman, came in and began to undress. She had betaken herself to that room about nine o'clock and had wished to take a candle with her ; but the stewardess had not allowed it, so she had lit her cigar by the lamp of the stewardess and, as the latter told us, had been smoking and drinking brandy and water there in the dark. However, about one o'clock, when my eyes were half shut, I saw her return into the cabin and begin to undress; but having fumbled about for some time unsuccessfully endeavouring to do so, she scrambled into her berth, as she was, with her clothes on, and I went to sleep. I had not long enjoyed a refreshing rest, when I was waked by the noise of my little brother coughing and choking; I listened for some time, and then got down from my berth and took him out of his bed. He coughed and seemed to be choking as if he had the croup; but, at last, he fell asleep, and I laid him in his bed again: but he had not been there one minute before his coughing returned; and he continued coughing and choking for two hours, but waked up whenever I attempted to put him in his bed. So I wrapped myself and him in shawls, and we slept together in the rocking chair till morning. Two of my sisters woke and asked what was the matter, and then went to sleep again. The little Irish baby woke up and began to cry, but soon was quieted: his mother

CHAP. VI.—LAKE ERIE. 151

and the old lady prescribed several remedies, some of which were in our medicine chest; but I could not give anything without asking mama, and I did not know her cabin. I was glad to arise in the morning from my unrefreshing sleep; hoping that I might pass the next night in a comfortable bed."

What think you, reader, of a night so passed in a steamboat on Lake Erie by the delicate, slim, young girl whom you may have known in far other scenes? While she was chatting or was dancing with you last winter, amid the gay and the highborn of those who thronged her mother's drawing-rooms in the handsomest palace in Rome, I warrant me she often thought with pleasure of her night on Lake Erie; as I trust my wife and my other children often think of the still harder and more menial offices to which we shall see them all hereafter so lovingly and so gallantly bow themselves. Thus do I testify my gratitude to them; hereafter, I may tell the cause of our so "roughing it."

" Why it is evident that they were travelling without any servants!"

Gentle reader! it was even so. While we lived at Talence, in France, only two of our servants, a lady's maid and a nurse, were English; and these had returned home, as they were unwilling to venture across the Atlantic. The others, women and men, were all French; and, of course, unsuited to such a journey. We had the less regretted losing our English servants because we knew that, in all probability, they would be sea sick and useless on the voyage, where stewardesses and stewards would supply their place; and would leave us to marry and settle in the United States soon after our arrival. At New York, we had been much put out by the treacherous desertion of the maid whom we had hired there; for although one attendant would have been little amongst our party, still she might have sufficed while in the two steamers and two railway cars that alone, as we thought, interposed between us and a more settled domicile. She, however, had failed us; and I had yet to learn the impossibility of finding servants in the western states. There were, also, other reasons which induced us to risk the journey without our usual travelling establishment. The time is not yet come when I may declare them... But declared they shall hereafter be. . . .

Next morning, our steamer was steadily proceeding westward through its quiet inland sea. The steamboats on these lakes recommend themselves as being " low pressure"—perhaps the people are more nervous than elsewhere, owing to their nearness to Canada; and we were only advancing at the rate of ten miles an hour. On our right hand, was a waste of waters; on our left, at no great distance, were the shores of New York State, now fading behind us, of Pennsylvania and of Ohio. There was nothing marked in the scenery of either. Hills, covered with forests amongst which were occasional clearings and farms, occasional villages, occasional towns, rose gently from the water edge—almost a regular bank. We passed the headland on which stands the little town of Erie, and in the harbour of which, in 1813, according to American boast, they built, in seventy days from the time when they were waving in their native forests, a fleet which contended successfully with the British on these waters. We stopped at Cleveland, where most of our passengers left us to proceed by railway to the interior of Ohio or to Pittsburgh. And here, in fact, we ourselves ought to have landed; but I had, in a great degree, taken my route from the maps and descriptive works on board the *Kate Hunter* and from Appleton's guide-book; and all these, having been printed during the preceding year, were already out of date; a railroad had been since made from Cleveland, of which they gave no notice. Guide books in the United States should be published every month, like Bradshaw's railway time tables!

But a fresh breeze came down from the great lakes and hills of North Canada, and tempered the noon-day heat; and pleasantly we walked or sat about the decks, as we advanced farther and farther to the west. Some strawberries which I had purchased as we stepped on board at Buffalo, were gratefully eaten in the " Bride's room". The basket that held them is painted, and bright-varnished in England,—a memorial of other lands. Then our children came to us in a body for instructions how they should meet the questioning and cross-questioning to which they had been subjected ever since they landed at New York. Young and old, parents and children, poor and rich,—all thought themselves entitled to ask "Where do you come from?" "Where are you going?" "How long have you been in the country?" "How long are you going to stop?" "I calculate your father will be for buying a location?" "Is not it an everlasting great country?" "How many brothers and sisters are you?" "Are you all one family?"—this doubt seemed to weigh upon the mind of all we met; large families are not common in the United States. Our children complained that a civil answer only brought on a more impertinent question; and besought us to tell them how they should meet their inquisitors. I considered a moment, and then desired them to answer very politely, but very innocently, either "I do not know," or else "You had better ask papa and mamma."

The plan succeeded. Cuddie Headrig in "Old Mortality," said that it was very useful to be able to look stupid; and our children thus got rid of many tormentors.

We were now on the high track followed generally by the agricultural emigrants to the West; to Michigan, Wisconsin, and the northern parts of Illinois. They can come up to Buffalo by the canal or railroad, as we had done; and thence find unbounded water carriage by the Great lakes; even a ship canal from Michigan to the Mississippi river enables them to go down it to New Orleans, and circumnavigate the greater part of the settled portion of the continent of North America. I myself had been strongly recommended to settle my sons in the State of Ohio on lands that should have been already partially cleared; while others again reminded me that, by so doing, I should allow the pioneer to reap the first great benefit of emigration; and should have to sink capital in paying him for improvement that the emigrant himself finds amusement, excitement, and profit in making for himself. All this was to be investigated. I myself had a fancy for the State of Indiana;

perhaps, because I had never been able to find out anything about it. At all events, we would go for a time to Cincinnati; see all Ohio, traverse Indiana and Illinois; and then, making St. Louis our head-quarters for a few months, attempt an excursion into Iowa, a new State which I had heard very highly spoken of.

Travelling as we did, I spent my time in conversing with people of all classes; and having in view the one object, to become thoroughly acquainted with the United States, I acquired a fund of information which I scarcely know how to condense; though I collated and methodised it at the time, and rejected all that I believe was not to be depended on.

The stewardess on board this Erie steamer was much interested in our large family; and behaved to my children with great attention and civility. She took us to be emigrants, as we represented ourselves; and told of the many others whom her steamer had conveyed to the Far West, and who were now settled in comfort and affluence. She made us laugh, by an account she gave of one English family who had lately passed back again, and returned to England, after a trial of only two months, disgusted with something that had displeased them. Poor people! we laughed at them; and little thought what we ourselves should be doing within the same period.

I must now copy Louie's statement.

" We arrived at six o'clock in the evening at Sandusky City, a large straggling place, something between a town and a village, with a very scanty population and ill-built houses. We went immediately to the hotel, a large handsome building, called the Townsend House; but I felt a cold chill creep over me as I saw the bedroom destined for four of us girls. It was a large room, with four bare white-washed walls, and but little furniture besides a couple of double beds covered with musquito curtains,—the first I had seen since I left my beloved Italy. Three large windows, in which almost every pane of glass was either cracked or broken, did not tend to make the room more cheerful and inviting. We were tired with our day at Niagara the day before; and Lucy and some of us had had little sleep during the night in the steam packet; and we retired to rest as soon as we had filled the places of the broken panes with towels as well as we could. We attempted to let down our musquito curtains; but, at the first touch, they fell, not being securely fastened. Not a single window-sash fitted into its frame; papa said they had been all made of green fir wood, which had shrunk; there were no weights and pulleys to raise them by, but pegs that were put into holes under the raised sash, as we have since found to be the general plan in the backwoods. Next morning, after breakfast, as two of my sisters were looking out of the window, the sash fell and hurt them; they narrowly escaped dying by the guillotine in America!

"In short," she continues, "it was with no feelings of regret that we quitted this very disagreeable place, and set off in the cars for Cincinnati, the " Queen city of the west", and one of the few towns in the United States of America which English people know, or care to know, anything about. Indeed, since our return to the " old country", I have been surprised and disappointed at the utter want of interest displayed by our country people on the subject of America. They seem to consider North America as a great desert, in which there are five or six large towns, such as New York, Cincinnati, Philadelphia, Boston, and Baltimore. As to South America, it is another large desert, peopled with parrots and monkeys, and containing silver mines. And this ignorance is the more surprising, because now so many people visit the western hemisphere, and write descriptions of their travels. Of the government and constitution of the country, every state of which is as large as all England and Scotland, and has independent laws, and a president of its own,—of all this, they know nothing: it is Hebrew to them."

Pretty strenuous criticism this of my daughter! However, we must not question the experience of a young lady whose thirteenth birthday had occurred when we were on board the *Kate Hunter*, and who wrote down her impressions a year and a-half afterwards.

I accompanied my luggage to the station-house at Sandusky, and found again here the same inconvenient plan of labelling and ticketing luggage, which I had first seen adopted at Albany, and which is general throughout the States: a brass token, with a number engraved upon it, is sewn to a leathern thong, and tied to each article, the owner of which is expected to put another brass token, engraved with the corresponding number, into his pocket. This the owner of one or two packages could easily do; but the custom-house officer at New York had counted forty-two packages as belonging to me; and it was no pleasant matter to have to find pocket-room for forty-two brass tokens as large as penny pieces. Then at the end of every journey, when the luggage was to be reclaimed, every holder of a token had to produce it as the number on the corresponding one tied to each trunk was called out; and as, of course, the numbers did not follow one another regularly, a most perplexing scene of confusion and delay always arose when any passenger had more than one or two packages.

I in vain endeavoured to make them understand the plan of fixing one and the same letter to all the luggage of one and the same owner, which might be reclaimed by the production of one check. They then declared that they could not understand me. I have no doubt they have adopted the plan since. They have no revered antiquated prejudices to prevent improvement.

But we were seated in cars like those I have before described, and were advancing along the " Lake Erie and Mad River Railroad". I regret that I can give no appropriate description of the " Mad River"; but, truth to say, I could never find it, see it, or hear of even its locality. The train passed onwards through forests of Scotch fir trees of no great size; nature has set them so close together, and the soil is so poor, that their growth is stunted. Striking at first, the effect soon became monotonous. The electric telegraph was conducted beside the railway: and our chief interest was soon derived from watching the many birds that perched upon its wires, of plumage and shape different from those of

Europe. Stray clearings appeared among the woods here and there; where the soil was a little better, the trees had been destroyed, and a few acres brought into cultivation; and a frame farmhouse might be seen on some slight elevation amid the forest in the distance. But such spots were few and far between; fir woods stretched darkly on every side, and no fence separated them from the line of the railway. The driver's whistle was, however, often and oftener heard; I marvelled what could cause such frequent warnings; and at length discovered that stray cattle were lying across the rails, and as the country became more inhabited, of course these became more frequent. About once in two hours, the trains stopped to take in a supply of wood fuelling; this was kept neatly cut and piled under sheds beside the log or frame cottage of the wood-cutter.

Dost know the difference, reader, between a log and a frame-house? The latter is, as its name implies, a framework of sawn timber, covered over with weather boards, like most of the barns and farm buildings in the south of Hampshire; the log-house is made of the whole boles or stems of trees laid one upon the other, and the one rudely "tenanted" into the other at the four corners. On the inside, the interstices between the boles are filled up with straw or clay. The frame-house is always painted white to preserve the boards; the log-house is generally whitewashed for neatness sake.

Whenever the trains stopped, as I have said, to take in wood, boys came into the cars with great jugs of lemonade and iced water, of which almost every passenger took a draught. Iced water and ice, the commonest necessary of the poorest as of the richest throughout the United States, is a luxury that may be said to be unattainable even to the wealthy in Europe. When the next station was a town, these water boys offered us cards and handbills recommending the several hotels in it.

But we were rising on the higher ground that parts the waters that flow into Lake Erie from those that incline southwards towards the Ohio River. The soil was better in quality; the country gave evidence of being more settled; fences began to hedge in the clearings from the railway; the guard's whistle was more seldom in requisition to arouse the cattle, sheep, or horses that had strayed from the forests and laid themselves to sleep on our line. Reader, if thy dwelling is in the country, desire a hedge-carpenter to put up for thee in thy grounds a wood fence without posts or nails, and mark how the poor man will stare! To fix up a timber fence without posts or nails! Impossible! And yet the land of the United States, where it is fenced at all, is fenced in by such. I desired my three daughters, from whose memoranda I occasionally quote, to write a description of a " worm fence ", as it is called, in the fewest possible words. That given by Lucy was unintelligible; Agnes covered her page with sketches and drawings, which are inadmissible here; Louie wrote as follows: " a number of poles are laid with the ends crossing one another in a zigzag line on the ground; others are laid on them again in the same manner, and so on until the fence is of a sufficient height. Its appearance is not unlike a half unfolded screen." I cannot improve upon this description. The poles of which it is formed are either small firs, or oak flitterns, split into two or four. They are about twelve or fourteen feet long, and are laid almost at right angles, the ends projecting a foot or two beyond where they lap over. It is evident that the rise can only be gained by the opening between each layer of poles, the width of which opening is dependent upon the thickness of the poles themselves. The fences are generally about twelve bars or poles high. The consumption of wood in such a fence appears, therefore, at first, to be three times as much as it would be in a four-rail English fence; but when we measure the extra quantity required on account of the zig-zag lines in which it is necessarily placed, and by the lapping over at the two ends of each rail, we find that the length of fencing, necessary to enclose the same space, is double what it would be if laid straight; so that, in real fact, six times as much wood has to be cut, split, hauled and built up as would be required to make the four rails of one of our straight fences. But an American will tell you that he saves the posts; that he saves the labour of digging holes in which to plant them; that he saves the labour of cutting mortices in which to insert the rails, or of shaping and nailing them; that the timber is worse than worthless to him, as he wishes to get rid of it; and that, during the winter, he can do little else. Jonathan is a shrewd calculator and, I daresay, he is right in this instance. According to his own proverb, " America will be an everlasting great country when it is all fenced!"

I now began to study the agriculture of the lands I passed through with great interest; not only on account of my views for the settlement of my children, but also as an amateur and practical agriculturist; for I had been called away from our home unexpectedly, for reasons that will hereafter be told, and, at this very time, I kept in hand and farmed by my bailiffs about two thousand acres of our estates in different counties of England. I was, therefore, competent to form an opinion on what I saw.

The soil, as I have said, improved greatly as we advanced into the interior of the State of

Ohio; we had left the fir forests and entered a country of fine oak timber; and the clearings were consequently more frequent, although in different stages of progress. In some, the trees had been hewn down and left on the ground to decay. In others, an attempt had been made to burn them: their smaller boughs had indeed been burnt off; but there stood the blackened trunks, throwing out the stumps of their great charred limbs in angry desolation. In some places, the plough was at work, amid stumps as thick as ninepins, turning and twisting about as only an American plough can. In others, the stumps had been partially dug up, and the ploughman could sometimes draw a straight furrow. In some places, separate fields were even enclosed by worm fences, and all the stumps had been grubbed up and cleared away, or at least they lay amid the corn ready to be drawn off next winter; a few great trees being left here and there for ornament. This showed that immense progress had been made; that the farmer had had spare capital to lay out, and that he was employing it with spirit; while, at the same time, he had an eye to the beautiful, and would not denude his location of all timber. But the spirit of progress, the spirit of money-making was at work; and in the more cultivated and improved parts of all, even these last memorials of the primeval forest had received notice to quit. They had been ringed, as we woodcutters say in England; the bark had been stripped all round from their great boles just above the earth; their boughs were bare; no leaves intercepted the sun and air from the crops beneath; and there they stood in their giant nakedness, the last of their race, and soon to topple over at the feet of the conquering intruder.

Meanwhile, the residence of the conqueror rose upon the field of his triumph, or beside the forest that still stood untouched, and covering, probably, nine-tenths of his farm. Small frame houses, neatly painted white, with green Venetian blinds, dotted the country pleasantly. Sometimes rising at a distance upon some elevation amid the forest, and surrounded closely by square farm buildings, they looked like gentlemen's seats from the old country, " bosomed high in tufted trees " of an ancestral park. But, in general, new buildings were placed near the railroad, as affording the easiest means of communication; some few were of brick; but frame building was preferred as cheaper and quite as durable. Bricks are badly made in the backwoods, and fall to pieces within half a century.

At Bellefontaine—why the place has such a pretty name, I know not; but at Bellefontaine, Yellow Springs, (where are some mineral baths,) and Xenia, the country is very pleasing. I cannot say beautiful and picturesque; for the forest produces a strange effect, and appears to level the landscape by filling up the hollows, and hiding all the broken ground. One would have supposed that, as it mantles the hills as well as the valleys, the relative elevation and depression would have been the same. The effect, however, is quite different; and looking at the clearings amongst the woods, we are surprised to see a prettily-undulating country where all around seems to be level. From Bellefontaine to Xenia, the soil is a rich loam; I was told that it improved even towards Columbus, the capital of the state: a fine

CHAP. VI.—LAKE ERIE.

country for the agriculturist. For here are no swamps, no rich bottoms to breed fever and ague: but what, in England, we should call a good barley and wheat land. The crops, however, were wonderfully slight; rarely did I see a wheat crop that would average four sacks to the acre; many were there that could hardly be cut and collected together from amid the stumps and offshoots springing up from imperfectly grubbed roots. The corn crops, (Indian corn), were very promising; but I thought to myself that we English landowners need not fear the competition of wheat imported from the United States.

We dined comfortably, and refreshed at different places on the way. At Xenia, we were delayed sometime, waiting for the train from Cleveland, through Columbus, to Cincinnati. By this line of country, we ought, in fact, to have come; but, as I have said, the books of last year could not tell us of it, as the railway did not then exist; and, in truth, we were beyond all guide-book information. The Cleveland and Columbus road had carried off most of the traffic through Sandusky; and our railway had, therefore, been allowed to get somewhat out of repair. We were a good deal shaken, though not "snaked" as sometimes happens; when the iron hooping that is nailed to sleepers, in some instances, for the cars to run on instead of rails, when this iron hooping becomes detached, and curling itself up, enters through the floor of a car and twists itself on and on amongst or through the passengers, missing or spitting them like larks, till it goes out at the other end or through the roof. We were not snaked; and we consoled ourselves for the jolting and slowness of our train, by considering that, owing to the competition, we had been brought from Buffalo to Sandusky, and from Sandusky to Cincinnati, a distance of four hundred and fifty-eight miles, for three dollars, or twelve shillings and sixpence a-head: state saloons, "bride's room", eating on board, and first class railway all included.*

* This calculation would be exact had we all paid as grown up passengers. But all through this journey, seven of us were considered as children, and, therefore paid half-price only. The father, mother, and eleven children, travelled as nine and a half grown persons—Louie and Agnes being classed among the babies.

From Xenia, where the Columbus train joined us, we went on more rapidly; but the cars were more crowded; we were getting tired; the evening closed in; and we could only occasionally get glimpses of water gliding swiftly in the starlight amid high banks and overhanging trees. This, we were told, was the Little Miami river; and that the scenery about it was pretty. Porters and boys of every size soon made an irruption into the cars, recommending different hotels in Cincinnati. I selected one who wore a label showing that he belonged to the far-famed Burnet House hotel; and I was assured, by some gentlemanly fellow-passengers who had kindly given me much information, that I might trust him with my forty-two brass checks with which to claim my baggage. The cars at length stopped; omnibuses, the only conveyances at the station, were in waiting from each hotel; that of the Burnet House was filled before I could collect my party, and we had to await its return. It came, and, for this second trip, we had it all to ourselves. "It was," writes Lucy, who had never seen the inside of an omnibus before, "like a very respectably-fitted up covered waggon, with cushions on the benches which ran all round it."

Thoroughly tired, we were set down at the foot of the handsome flight of steps leading up to the Burnet House hotel, where I had to pay the porter three and a half dollars for bringing my luggage from the station; or two-and-sixpence more than I had paid for the carriage and food of myself for the last four hundred and fifty-eight miles.

We were all soon asleep in not very comfortable rooms.

CHAPTER VII.

CINCINNATI.

The Burnet House hotel.—The Queen City of the West.—Bill of fare in Ohio.—The cathedral.—The Catholics.—The author's politico-religious creed.—The calendar.—The ecclesiastical seminary.—The upper crust of Cincinnati.—Search for a location.—Porkopolis.—The ladies' saloon.—Honorary titles.—The banker.—Hours of business.—Engravings on paper money.

We had not been able to get to bed until two hours and a-half after midnight; and we arose this morning dissatisfied with our rooms, and resolved to change them or the hotel. When we went down to breakfast, we could not but admire the arrangement and architecture of the building, which was more like a church on the outside, and a London club house within, than like an hotel according to European notions. It was nothing very extraordinary in the United States: although in the first-class of hotels even there. A broad flight of steps, in the middle of a lofty basement, surrounded with a stone balustrade, led up to a large building three, four, and five stories high, with a centre and double wings; the centre, which was five stories high, was again surmounted by a dome and lantern, from which rose a flag-staff bearing a wide banner. The inside arrangement corresponded with the outside; the entrance hall was good; the stairs were good. The ladies' drawing-rooms were large and very handsomely fitted up. The carpets in most of these hotels and steamboats are peculiarly rich.

We had been told that breakfast could be had from seven to ten o'clock. We were, therefore, rather late, and breakfasted alone in a large, handsome eating room; waited upon by a dozen free blacks, in snow-white jackets, who received us with that ease and politeness, which is so peculiar to the free blacks of the United States. I will not say that they seem to be *the* gentry of America; but certainly their manners have a suavity and *prevenance*, on the absence of which the Irish and German waiters seem to pride themselves.

After breakfast, I wished to make some arrangement for other rooms, and to settle the price at which my family was to be boarded: but here I was met by the inconvenience of these great establishments. The proprietor could not personally attend to everything and every one; perhaps he did not attend to anything or any body; and his authority was delegated to clerks and waiters, who were either fussy or indifferent. I found no great wish to oblige in the matter of the bed-rooms, and a saucy independence as to the terms. The waiters ran off hither and thither,—too busy to attend to a mere Britisher with his wife and eleven children. I left them and walked out.

I threaded a number of streets, drawn at right angles, most of which were paved in the centre and had side pavements of brick, shaded by rows of small sycamore trees. Business took me to a Colonel ——. I had no letter of recommendation to him; but he filled some public department on which I wished for information, and I introduced myself to his office. He received me with a frankness and an evident wish to be of service, which an Englishman would have thought derogatory to himself; but the Americans seem to be a thoroughly good-natured and good-hearted people. He gave me all the information I needed, and then said, "But I had heard of you before. Some friends of mine came home in the cars last night, and they told me of a great British family that had arrived. Where are you located?"

I told him at the Burnet House, when he lifted up his hands, and said, "Well now, I guess that you had better get out of that before the day is out. Why, you will be ruined! I don't know what your means are; but, whatever they are, with all those children, and one more whom you say is coming from England, you must have something else to do with your money than to squander it in hotels. It is an excellent house, mind; a fashionable house; I myself should certainly go to it, if I had need to go to any hotel in Cincinnati, and were alone; but I would never think of taking my lady and family there. Go and look out for another hotel directly."

We shook hands; and I went and called on another friend, who gave me the same advice.

CHAP. VII.—CINCINNATI.

The town of Cincinnati, in the year 1800, contained a population of seven hundred inhabitants: in 1840, its population was forty-seven thousand: in 1850, it was one hundred and sixteen thousand. It is built on the right bank of the Ohio river; and is about one thousand miles from New York and from Boston; or, as one ought now to reckon distances, sixty-seven hours. It stands upon a double platform gently rising from the river; and is again surrounded by a wall of lofty and picturesque hills that appear immediately beyond its streets. Some of the streets run up the sides of these hills: and in them, I was informed, reside the " upper crust" of the society of Cincinnati. The broad stream of the Ohio circles round the base of the mountains and of the town; and two suburbs, containing about twenty thousand inhabitants, rise on its opposite bank—though that bank be in the slave state of Kentucky. Floating wharves are adapted to the rise and fall of the river, so that merchandise can, at all times, be landed and embarked without difficulty. Steam-boats line its quays and cover its waters. About one hundred and fifty are owned by merchants of the town. The imports of Cincinnati are worth fifty millions, her exports fifty-six millions of dollars a-year: and upwards of two hundred steam engines are at work in flour mills, saw mills, cotton foundries, type foundries, etc.

For the "Queen City of the West" is not merely a commercial place; it is a seat of literature also. There are published here eleven daily and twenty-five weekly newspapers, and six monthly periodicals. Book business, printing and stereotyping are done here with beauty and neatness.

We have all heard of the learned pig. Hog slaughtering and pork packing is the next important of all the trades of Cincinnati. They have slaughter and packing houses which enable them to dispose of twenty thousand hogs per day; but as the weather necessarily restricts the season to about twelve weeks, and as there must be many unpropitious days even in these, they can seldom get through more than four hundred thousand hogs a-year!

Nor is religion forgotten by the inhabitants

of Cincinnati. Sixty churches are devoted to different modes of worship. Of these, twelve are Catholic; two are Jewish; four are episcopal; the others are dedicated to the promulgation of what, in England, are called different modes of dissent. In nine churches, the service is performed in German.

A busy, smoking, reeking place Cincinnati thus very necessarily appeared to us during this first morning's walk; the sun was very hot; and I found the air impregnated with an oppressive odour which I could not understand. We returned to the Burnet House to dinner at two o'clock. About one hundred people were seated in the dining room: the women were, as a matter of course in America, very stylishly and flauntingly drest: many of the men sat in brown holland frock coats. A crowd of black waiters were in attendance and guided us to our places. Beside my plate, I found a printed sheet, which I copy verbatim, though I cannot give the engraving of the hotel which headed it:

BURNET HOUSE.
A. B. COLEMAN, PROPRIETOR.

HOURS FOR MEALS.

Breakfast.................... 7 to 10 | Tea 6
Dinner—Gents' ordinary ...   1 | Supper ...... 9 to 12
Ladies' ordinary ...   2½ |

☞ Servants and children—Breakfast at 7 ; Dine at 1 ; and Tea at 6.

☞ PRIVATE SERVANTS NOT ALLOWED IN THE ORDINARIES.

☞ Children occupying seats at table will be charged full price.

☞ All meals, lunches, &c., sent to rooms will be charged extra.

BILL OF FARE.

☞ No gong will be sounded for breakfast.

SOUPS.

Vermicelli soup.   Chicken soup with crust.

BOILED DISHES.   ROAST DISHES.
Ham.   Pork, apple sauce.
Corned Beef.   Beef.
Tongues.   Lamb, mint sauce.
Jole and Cabbage.   Spring Chickens.
Chickens and Pork.   Phipps Ham, champagne sauce.

Calf's Head, brain sauce.   Broiled Sweetbreads with Pork.
Chicken Salads.   Baked Pork and Beans.

CHAP. VII.—CINCINNATI.

SIDE DISHES.

Lamb cutlets in paper.
Fillets of Pork with Asparagus.
Charlotte of Apples, French style.
Minced Salt Fish Baked.
Breast of Lamb, Breaded.
Blanquettes of Veal in a Border of Potatoe.
Kidneys on a Form of Bread.
Macaroni in Forms and Plain.
Veal cutlets, Italian style.
Stewed Lamb with fine vegetables.
Pies Garnished with Poached Eggs.
Croquettes of Beef Tongue.
Fricasseed Chicken with Peas.
Ragout of Mutton with Asparagus.

RELISHES.

Pickles.	Lettuce.	Horse Radish.
Rhubarb sauce.		Cucumbers.

VEGETABLES.

Boiled Potatoes.	Boiled Rice.
Onions.	Cabbage.
Beets.	Homony.
Peas.	

PASTRY.

Currant Pies.	Pumpkin Pies.
Custard Pudding.	Charlotte Kisses.
Iced Lemon Cakes.	Almond Kisses.

DESSERT.

Almonds.	Raisins.	Prunes.
Strawberries.	Pecan Nuts.	Hickory Nuts.
	Ice Cream.	

Thursday, June 12, 1851.

What thinkest thou, reader, of a dinner in the back woods of America, one thousand miles from Boston or New York? The cooking of the dishes, such as they were, was very good; and the waiting excellent. On the reverse side of the Bill of Fare, was printed a list of wines, with prices: port, sherry, and Madeira, about double what they would be in England; champagne, claret, and Rhine wines, about the same as on the continent of Europe. But not one person in twenty drank anything but iced water: the others took champagne. The early dinner hour of America precludes drinking; and to sit more than twenty minutes at table would interfere with business.

After dinner, we moved to the Walnut Street House, a large hotel in a more quiet and airy part of the town, that had been much recommended to me, and where they engaged to board us for a week at half the charge made by the Burnet House people. On the following day, I received a message from the latter, intimating that, if I would return to them, they would be glad to take us in on terms which, had they proposed them before, I should have assented to. It was now too late. We were well satisfied with the Walnut Street House. We had not the "ice" and the "kisses" of the other bill of fare; but our table was well supplied, and our younger children were all allowed to dine with us; this was very soothing to the dignity of the elder of them, and was a satisfactory change to all.

In the map or plan of Cincinnati, I had seen a large space marked as "The Cathedral". I made my way towards it, and found that it was a Catholic church. While in England, I had corresponded with Archbishop Purcell: telling him my plans for my boys, and that I had thoughts of sending some of them to be educated in the country of their future home. I had been much pleased by the interest he had very kindly expressed in them. I now regretted to find that His Grace was himself in Europe; but his brother, the Very Reverend Edward Purcell, was at home, and received me with open arms,—with Irish warmth and American frankness. He showed me over the cathedral, which was, as my Guide Book said, a very handsome building: being two hundred feet long, by eighty feet broad, and sixty feet high. Inside, the effect is very chaste, simple, and imposing. A noble altar, of pure Carara marble, stands in its place at the west end. A few good paintings adorn the walls. The roof is supported by handsome Corinthian pillars. The order of the exterior architecture is less defined; Mr. Purcell insisted that it was American; it had a lofty spire, and was, altogether, a very creditable and handsome pile.

The Catholic religion was making immense progress in the state of Ohio. About one-half of the population of Cincinnati is Catholic. Besides the twelve Catholic churches in the town, seven others were in its immediate vicinity; and the religion seemed to be going a-head quite as much as everything else in the country. The archbishop himself being an American, and a man of business and of zeal tempered by prudence and liberality, was highly spoken of by all the people of the state, and they seemed to be proud of him as a countryman. His reverend brother partakes his views, and admirably seconds them.

For however timidly the Catholic hierarchy in Europe may have allied itself to civil governments, and have allowed itself to be considered the upholder of despotism and the foe to progress, Catholics in America are able to declare, as M. de Montalembert has declared in France, that there is nothing in the spirit of their religion opposed to the spirit of freedom; that the fullest civil rights may be asserted and exercised by the most devotional mind; and that religion and temporal policies are quite independent the one of the other. In the United States of America, all religions have a fair field and no favour; and Catholics there ask for nothing more. Where no man is taxed to support what he believes to be another man's error, religious charity only can lead one man to interest himself in the religious opinions of another man. The fire of religious discord must lack fuel where no religion can boast of state patronage. Nations and bodies of men do not quarrel or fight to get to heaven, but for the loaves and fishes to be eaten on the road, or for the full liberty of going thither by whichever road they fancy— or elsewhere. The political principles of the United States are in accordance with these convictions; and amid such, the Catholic faith prospers.

" Deorum injuriæ Diis curæ—Let the gods avenge their own wrongs," wisely said Tiberius.

" Let each one mind his own affairs and pay for his own priest and doctor if he wants one," says the statesman.

" Agreed," assents the religionist: " I agree that the State shall look upon us as citizens only; that it shall have no right to inquire, and shall not inquire what are our individual opinions, or whether we believe ourselves even to have souls or not: but I myself do believe in one particular religion, and I think it my duty to try and persuade others to believe it also."

" Practice, teach, preach whatever you like," reiterates the statesman : " I, as a statesman, am not particularly inspired to know whether your opinions are right or wrong; and as a statesman merely, I do not care. It is no affair of mine—provided only that you do not disturb the public peace. If you do, I shall come down upon you all alike."

" Hurrah, for liberty of conscience!" cries the citizen.

" Magna est veritas et prevalebit—truth is great and it will prevail"! ejaculates the religionist.

" And, if it is not true, it ought not to prevail," concludes the philosopher.

The Queen City of the West has not, any more than Buffalo, arrived at that degree of civilisation which should have taught it to number its houses: and it is difficult to conceive the troublesome and intricate method of giving directions in use here. For example: you are told that you will find St. Xavier's church in " Sycamore Street, between Sixth and Seventh Streets:" such an one lives in " Main Street, between Court and Canal;" and another " in Race Street, between Thirteenth and Fourteenth Streets;" another, at " foot of Warren Street, near Fourth Street." We are told that the first thing the French allied army did on landing at Gallipoli was to paint names to the several streets and numbers on the houses. I hope the resident of the United States at Constantinople, after experiencing the improvement, will write home and recommend the plan to his countrymen.

I bought an almanac at Cincinnati, and referring to it, to see at what time the sun rose and set, I was certainly taken aback and startled by the evidence it afforded of the greatness of the country. Instead of one column, which is sufficient to give that intelligence in any state in Europe, four columns were here required for the same purpose! Thus, on 14th June 1851,

Calendar for BOSTON: N.England, N. York State, Michigan, Wisconsin and Iowa.		Calendar for N. YORK CITY, Conn.: New Jersey, Pennsylvan., Ohio, Indiana and Illi's.		Calendar for BALTIMORE, Virginia, Kentucky and Missouri.		Calendar for Charleston, N. Caroli.,Tenn., Geo., Alabama, Miss. and Louisiana.	
Sun rises	Sun sets	Sun rises	Sun sets	Sun rises	Sun sets	Sun rises	Sun sets
4.24	7.35	4.30	7.30	4.34	7.26	4.53	7.6

Truly it is a mighty country! The American eagle sits on the top of the Rocky Mountains and dips his beak in the Atlantic and his tail in the Pacific: he stretches one wing over

CHAP. VII.—CINCINNATI.

Canada the other over Mexico, and he holdeth the continent in his claws!

It was sad news to us, on arriving at Cincinnati, to find that Asiatic cholera was making its appearance again in the city. They had suffered from it severely in the preceding year. The papers, also, informed us that it was strong on the line of the Mississippi river; and this had made us the more anxious to halt at Cincinnati before we went on to St. Louis. I wished to make it my head quarters while studying the capabilities of the land of the neighbouring countries: and we looked out for a house in which to place our family. A furnished house could no more be rented here than at Bordeaux: nay, even unfurnished houses were not to be had. They cannot build them as fast as they are wanted for their own occupation. I inquired for one of the nice looking houses on the hills, in the outskirts of the town, with trim gardens about them, and which enjoyed splendid views: but I was informed that all those belonged to " the upper crust" of the town, and that they were not to be let. One, indeed, of these was offered to me; but I discovered that six people had died in it of the cholera during the last summer. The upper crust owner of this one puffed it, therefore, in vain.

My friend, the Very Rev. Edward Purcell, called on me in his buggy and took me out to see the ecclesiastical seminary that had been lately built by his brother, the archbishop. We passed out of the town and along a very dusty road, which, in other respects, was not a bad one, though occasionally mended with planks. We passed numerous tea-gardens, and rose among the hills. The scenery became very varied; the hills were steep and broken. We circled about them, to catch different points of view; and, at length, came to the Seminary. It was a large, handsome building, only just completed: as yet, it was unfurnished, uninhabited; the classes were not yet organised: all this was to be done when the archbishop should return from Europe. The rooms were very large and lofty. We passed through them all and out upon the shingle roof: for, be it known, that tiles and slates are here made of wood, which, being covered with gas tar, look as well as stone and, I believe, last a matter of thirty years. The masters of the vessels that trade from New York to Newfoundland or New Orleans, are said, by the captains of outward bound vessels, to drop such on the sea as they go along, in order that they may be able to find their way back again; as Jack the Giant Killer dropped marbles from his pockets.

The view from this seminary was magnificent. On the edge of one of the highest hills where they encircle Cincinnati, it overlooked pretty glens, to the right and left, and the whole of the busy, reeking city underneath; it overlooked the blue river winding between it and its opposite suburbs,—winding between the cultivated hills of Ohio and the green forest-clad mountains of Kentucky. It was a beautiful prospect.

I urged Mr. Purcell to allow me to rent and inhabit the seminary, that we might enjoy the views and the pure air that breathed around. We would furnish our floor, and surrender the whole so soon as it was needed for ecclesiastical purposes. He laughed off my request. I know not why he hesitated to grant it. Perhaps he thought that our plan of spending some time in America, and of settling our boys there, was a fancy that would soon pass away. "It would never suit your evident habits and ideas," he said to my wife. "The only chance of getting along for such as you, would be for you to go into a slave state. You will not find here the servants and the manners necessary to what you think your comforts."

Yet in his love and admiration of America and of the character of the natives, Mr. Purcell was enthusiastic. He declared them to be the most kind-hearted people in the world: passionate, to a degree that would terrify, but their anger soon wearing away. Religious? —that was their own affair: he spoke not as an ecclesiastic: the men had not time to think of religion: but they were without prejudices; frank; intelligent. He was fond of considering himself an American; although, in real fact, I believe he is Irish-born. He cannot be an American; otherwise, according to his own showing, he would have long since forgotten his anger against me for that I remonstrated with him for having removed my sons from college to college without my sanction or knowledge.

I made inquiries about the purchase of land; and was informed that the State no longer possessed any great quantity in Ohio: that all had been sold except some small portions in the north: and that the office for the sale of public lands had, therefore, been removed to Defiance, as being nearest to the tracts still undisposed off. The town of Defiance, however, is on the Maumee river, in a marshy and unhealthy part of the country; and, on this account, it was that these public lands still hung on hand.

I went to some of the many private estate agencies in Cincinnati and heard of several desirable locations, confirmatory of the opinion I had formed of the soil as I travelled in the railway cars from Sandusky. All agreed that the country about Chilicothe and on the Scioto River, flowing from Columbus to the Ohio, was as rich as any in North America: but all agreed, also, that the proprietors of it knew its value; and that it would cost as much per acre as good land in England.

I was pursuaded to go and see an estate somewhere near Cincinnati:—a most desirable, paying property, that was to be had very cheap. I hired a buggy and, with my wife, started to find it—being duly warned that, in driving, I was always to take and keep on the right side of the road. We left the town and were soon involved in a romantic ravine amid some beautiful hills. A steep ascent led us to the top of them, and we inquired for a Dr.——, I forget his name: but he had been described as "a very fine gentleman"; and we expected to find something quite " upper crust". We passed before a handsome building which, I was told, was the Ohio State Agricultural College; and, after inquiring at a pretty cottage surrounded by a garden, in which roses and vines, intertwined, shaded delicious arbours, we were directed to another, where we found a shabby little man, who got upon a shabby little horse and scampered wildly about for a quarter of an hour. At length, he returned with the Doctor, who was not unlike himself —except, perhaps, that he looked still more dirty and shabby. The two together harnessed the shabby little horse to a shabby little buggy, and whipped it away along a sandy road, desiring us to follow. They talked incessantly as I did so—asking every imaginable question: and though I did not quite do like my Frank, who, after we had told our children to reply to all inquiries that they did not know, told an inquisitive American that he did not know his own name, that he did not know where he came from, that he did not know who were his father and mother nor how many brothers and sisters he had—although, I say, I did not quite answer like Frank, I flattered myself that the Doctor and his friend got little out of me. I myself discovered that they were partners, and had taken the land in question in some business transaction for a bad debt.

We hastened on between worm fences and by various lanes; and, at length, pulled up by the road side. We were to dismount. This was the location. Where? The clearing and the woods behind, and the buildings. We clambered over the fences and inspected the farm buildings; one small barn and a shed, both falling to pieces. We made our way through the tangled weeds and briers that encumbered a young orchard, and over another fence into two or three ploughed fields. This was all the cleared land—about sixty acres.

There were some three hundred acres of wood; fine oak timber. All the soil was a good strong loam; rather too stiff. What was the price? The doctor and his friend had taken the whole at one hundred dollars per acre; they would sell all in one lot at one hundred and twenty dollars.

We returned to Cincinnati, and I reported to my friends what I had seen. They did not think there had been anything so cheap within six miles of the town.

"Cheap? why it comes to twenty-five pounds sterling per acre. What interest would it bring in?

" Interest! you must not exactly look to that. It is fine timber, and would almost pay the expense of cutting down and clearing the ground. You might get some interest for your money by growing vegetables and fruit for the town. But you must look to subdividing it; and to the increase in the value of all property. It will be worth twice as much in four years time. Oh, it is wonderfully cheap; and if you don't buy it, I think I shall."

I gave my friend full liberty to do so; as I had no intention either of setting up as a market gardener at Cincinnati, or of speculating on the improvement of property in the pig-killing metropolis.

For, at last, we had found out that the reeking stench, as of hot seething fat, which had annoyed and puzzled us since our arrival in Cincinnati, arose from the hog slaughter houses. Evening after evening, it was drawn up by the hot sun, and borne by the clammy breeze to our windows, where flies buzzed and enjoyed themselves. Fancy the steam that must arise in the hot summer weather even from empty houses in which twenty thousand hogs have been slaughtered each day in the winter! Faugh!

Meanwhile we were domesticating ourselves in our Walnut-street hotel, and were getting the people a little more into our ways. Husband and wife—more united than those of the continent of Europe—always occupy the same room and the same bed in the United States; and I had had some difficulty in persuading the porters that separate basins and ewers were needed for them. I succeeded at last, though with difficulty; for the porters and waiters were Irish emigrants, who, having doubtless spent their lives with the pig on a mud floor, all alike undefiled by water at home, felt that the carrying of water to our rooms impeded the digestion of the full meals that pampered their insolence in America. The Irish in Ireland may be the "finest peasantry in the world;" certainly the Irish in England show attachment, affection and gratitude to those who befriend or even treat them fairly; if such be the national character at home, it is wonderfully changed in its passage across the Atlantic. One would be inclined to think that, like wild animals, it can be only tamed by starvation; and that when once it has tasted meat and knows that it can never want again, its nature exhibits itself, like that of the cage-bred tiger when first it has lapped blood.

My second son, the eldest then with us, had a quarrel with an Irish housemaid in this hotel, which was near causing us to change our quarters. He was sitting one morning at the piano in the ladies' drawing-room, (and every ladies drawing-room, whether ashore or afloat in America, seems to have a piano in it, which is thumped upon by all who can play a dozen notes by heart), he was sitting at this piano, playing some little air, when this Irish housemaid ordered him not to touch it. A lad of sixteen naturally resented any order, still more an order so uncivilly given. A war of words ensued, when the wench called to the landlord, who was passing. My boy told him not to allow his servants to speak impertinently, and left the room. The landlord did so also, locking the door after him, and taking away the key. Soon after, my wife and two elder daughters, who had not heard of this squabble, came to the door, and finding it locked, sent for the key. The landlord appeared, and said that the ladies sitting-room was not intended for children. "But," said my wife, " I wish to sit there myself with my daughters; I presume it is for our use?"

"The room," replied Mr. Sweeny, "is for ladies to sit in when they are dressed to receive their visitors;" and, at the same time, he cast a rather supercilious look at the travelling dresses of our party.

I came in soon after, and was told what had happened. Of course, I went immediately to Mr. Sweeney, and gave the fellow, as the phrase is, a bit of my mind; as to himself, his guests, and those he had to deal with. The Scotchman, as I believe he was, though he tried to pass himself off for an American, stammered various excuses, and went and unlocked the door.

But the female vanity of "my womankind" had been insulted by the implied objection to their dress. They would no longer save the trouble of the Irish porter; and they made him carry up to their rooms three or four heavy chests and imperials. They could not, as Agnes said, put on "low light muslin or silk dresses, and sham gilt bracelets and rings; but they dressed themselves like English ladies, resident rather than travelling. The effect was magical upon the vulgar minds of our landlord and his crew; and it was impossible to meet with greater deference than we afterwards received.

When the master of Eton confided to Dr. Parr, that he feared a " barring out" among the boys, the latter advised him " to buy a large cocked hat—a tremendously large cocked hat", and quoted

> " Hi motus animorum atque hæc certamina tanta
> Pulveris exigui jactu compressa quiescent."

Ignorant human nature is the same, whether in Windsor forest or in the backwoods of America.

It was after this episode that a certain Captain Trumpbour, who sat in the bar-room and managed the hotel for the great Mr. Sweeney, came to me, and, with the greatest deference, begged to know how he ought to address me; he knew my name, he said; but it was not seemly in him to say only *Mister;* " was it Colonel, or General, or what?" I assured him that I had no claim to any title whatever. " It could not be! It ought not to be! Would not I assume one while travelling in the United States?" I told him that I should consider any title other than that of " Admiral" an affront; and, when he was hastening to bestow it on me, I disappointed him, by saying that it was not our practice to assume rank or office to which we were not entitled. I then turned the conversation by asking him if he himself were in the United States Navy, or whence he had the title of " Captain ", which, I observed, every one gave him?

For a month or two, he had commanded a steamboat on the Ohio between Cincinnati and Pittsburgh.

Messrs. Beebee of New York had given me, not an order on their correspondents here for the few thousand dollars I should want on the journey; but a receipt for the same and the name of their correspondent at Cincinnati. I went to the firm and found the head-partner, in a brown holland jacket and vest, behind the counter, chewing tobacco most vigorously, which he offered to me. I declined; and stood and watched the dexterity with which he counted over and examined a packet of dollar notes which a depositor was handing to him. He counted and examined them much more rapidly than any one unhabituated to the business could have counted them only: and as he quickly turned them over between finger and thumb, he threw out one, merely observing:—

" That's made by the wrong man."

The owner of the forged note took it up without one word of remark.

The banker was very busy then: and asked me if I could not call again after four o'clock. "The bank would be shut; but the door would be on the latch and they would be in attendance for less public business."

This I must record as one of the worst features in American domestic life,—every man is in business, and the business is never over. Nominally, the office may be shut; but, in reality, the merchant, or the lawyer, or the commission agent, is bound to be at the beck and call of whoever may want him. From the early morning until late at night, he is only permitted to snatch a quarter of an hour or twenty minutes, during which he may rush away to swallow his food: that feat accomplished, as Americans only can accomplish it, he must hurry back to his office to await the pleasure of some one who might just as well have called at an earlier hour. Under such a system, no domestic feeling, no domestic establishment is possible. The man of business can have no mornings and no evenings with his family. I know some in these western States who have attempted to adopt the European plan; who have given notice that their offices would be really closed at four or five o'clock: they were considered to be presumptuous and impertinent,—as setting themselves above their clients, and dictating at what hour they would earn their money. And others, in the same line of business, lacking the honour said to exist among thieves, the *esprit de corps*, or the spirit of combination which actuates Europeans, improved the discontent, and ran off with the business from their more refined and gentlemanly brethren.

I called again after four at the Cincinnati Bank; and, sure enough, partners and clerks were all at work; though the room was no longer crowded as in the morning. I showed Mr. Beebee's receipt, and they bought it of me at a premium of seven-eights. I asked how forged notes were to be known from others; and was assured that practice only would enable me to detect them. I was shown several forgeries, which I could not distinguish to be such even when placed beside those that were " made by the *right* man": but the banker pointed out some slight flaws that were sufficient for his practised eye. The signature of the issuer might seem perfect, but there was something different in the flourish of a letter, in the copper plate, or in the engraving of a hand of one of the figures. The paper money of the United States is very beautiful. It is for any sums from one dollar upwards—convertible into gold on demand at the bank that issues it: hence it maintains its nominal value. I have now before me a note of New York of the Manhattan Company: in the centre, is the figure of a water god—I presume Father Hudson, seated on one side of a river: a moody red Indian sits, sadly, facing him:

above, a European face uplifts a curtain and shows the river, covered with shipping moored to the quays of a large town in the distance. At one end of the note, is the portrait of an Indian chief in a headdress of cock's feathers and a necklace of shells : at the other, Justice with her scales, and Plenty with her horn are on each side of the American eagle. What could be more emblematic of the past and the present?

I have before me a New Hampshire note, which shows, in the centre, a beautifully-engraved representation of a railway train passing beside neat cottages and ploughed fields. On one side, the head of Palinurus ; on the other, a Plenty with cornucopia, plough, and wheatsheaf :—a well-engraved Durham ox is at the bottom. Here, again, is evidence of the tastes and aims of the community.

I have before me a note of a Maryland Bank. Here also is a remarkably well-executed centre engraving, showing a group of Indians—mother and child at rest on one side ; European children studying school-books and the globes on the other : both groups overshadowed by the broad shield, charged with the stripes and stars. At one end, is Justice standing beside shipping and merchandize, and holding sword, olive branch and scales; on the other, is a noble figure representing Architecture and her tools, with a porticoed building in the background: at the bottom, is a steam engine in full work. Here, too, we have emblems of the idle past and of the busy present.

Let me add that the ornamental scrollwork about all these notes is very beautiful.

I have before me a note of the midland district of Canada, " chartered by Act of Parliament." In the centre, is the ill-drawn figure of a great awkward Indian woman stepping from out her canoe amid swamps and forests. At one end, is a simpering face of Prince Albert in stars and uniform; at the other, the portrait of Her Gracious Majesty with crown on head—both being very bad likenesses very badly engraved; underneath, are the arms of England with lion and unicorn. These are emblems of the past, unchanged except by the dominion of England. No evidence of commerce, of agriculture, of arts, of science : North America, such as she was; but with England watching over her. I do not say that it is a true representation of the state of the country; I know that it is not so. But why is such an one given? Why cannot we, as well as the United States, avail ourselves of the means which the circulation of a "five shilling" note gives us to impart a lesson of hope, of energy, of improvement? Cannot we find as good artists to engrave our emblems? Cannot we, like them, tell our people to be industrious, to look to the future as well as to the past?

Comparing these different notes, it would really appear as if the order to design and engrave those for Canada had been given to some envious Yankee, who had availed himself of the opportunity to circulate a satire and a libel upon our territory.

CHAPTER VIII.

THE PLEDGE.

Father Mathew. — Another pledge. — The cathedral. — Mrs. Trollope. — Incendiarism.— Jesuits. — Cardinals.—American Catholics. — Irish emigrants. — The Maine liquor law. — Forward!

THE celebrated and rev. Father Mathew, the Irish Apostle of Temperance, was in Cincinnati when I arrived there; and the walls were placarded with handbills announcing that he would preach and deliver the Pledge at the cathedral on the following Sunday. He was a guest at the archbishop's residence; and I had been introduced to him on my first visit. One day I called on the Rev. Mr. Purcell and, not finding him at home, was shown into a parlour, to await his return: there I found Father Mathew sitting near the window, and his secretary at a desk on the other side of the room. He was a middle-sized man, of apparently about fifty-five years of age, with black hair sprinkled with grey, and a ruddy countenance. His manner was remarkably cold; courteous, but without polish. His enunciation very measured and slow. He was still suffering from the remains of a paralytic seizure that had affected him in one of the Southern States. This might have hindered, in some degree, his enunciation; but could not have produced that remarkable coldness of manner, so devoid of all the enthusiasm which one had expected to find in him. Yet it was thoroughly earnest. While we sat there, several persons came in to take the pledge: he spoke to them all kindly, gravely, but with chilling earnestness, if the expression can be allowed.

"Intoxicating drink is at the bottom of almost every sin and evil."

"Youth is the season of good resolutions."

These and similar phrases, he repeated to all, intermingled with a few words of inquiry. Most of those who came in, were Americans; most of them, Protestants. One party of three or four American Protestant young men, who seemed to be of a superior class, called in amongst others. All took the pledge, and the secretary

CHAP. VIII.—THE PLEDGE.

inscribed the names of all in his books. Some begged to have medals; and, to these, the secretary handed them at cost price. Father Mathew was said to have spent his all in medals and papers which he distributed gratis as long as he had the means of procuring them: he was now obliged to make his pledged ones pay for them; but they were not offered to any who did not ask for them.

I and my wife had to sit here long, waiting for Mr. Purcell; and we kept up a desultory conversation broken by these applicants to the reverend gentleman. He said that he had enrolled nearly three millions of teatotallers since he had been in the United States, and hoped to complete that number before he returned to Europe. His secretary talked more than he did; and seemed rather to make light of his patron's earnestness.

"Father Mathew," I exclaimed at length, "you and we shall all lose our characters!"

"How so, sir?" he solemnly inquired.

"Every one will know that we have been sitting with you for an hour; and they will say that your reverence needed all that time before we could persuade my wife to take the temperance pledge."

Not a muscle of his face moved as she laughingly added, "How should I get back to Europe, if I did? Brandy and water was the only thing that checked sea sickness on my voyage out."

"There is one pledge, Father Mathew," I said in the hope of rousing him; "there is one pledge that I wish you could get American women to take."

"What is that, sir?" he asked with some slight look of supercilious interest.

"I wish you could make them pledge themselves not to spend more in dress than their fathers or husbands could afford."

"A matter of quite minor importance!" he exclaimed scornfully.

"Do you think so?" I said. "You cannot have travelled through the United States without noticing, as I have, the extravagant, expensive dresses of all the females:—I do not speak of the free negresses, in their white muslin dresses, white satin shoes, and green silk parasols to preserve their complexions;—let them dress on Sundays as they will, for the present: but you must be aware that every American woman, whatever be her position in life, spends two or three times as much on her dress as one in the same station would spend in England. Do not you see the long train of evil which must follow from this rage for the vanities of dress ?"

"Not to be compared to the evils of drink," he insisted.

Mr. Purcell came in, and I asked him what seats we could have in the cathedral where we might see and hear Father Mathew.

" Seats !" he exclaimed: " the church only holds five thousand sittings. There is not a chance of your finding even standing room. But come through this house; and my housekeeper will lead you to a private gallery."

We did so on the following morning, and were excellently well placed. The mighty organ pealed: the congregation seemed most devotional: the usual holy service was performed with decorum and solemnity. When it was over, the whole body of the clergy left the building: nor did they return. Not the smallest sacristan or chorister boy was there in surplice, to intimate that what was to follow was part of the service of the church, or that the clergy sanctioned it. The lights were extinguished and the altar was left bare. Father Mathew came forward before it, and began his discourse. His utterance was impeded, as I had observed before: he spoke of the illness he had endured and from which he still suffered, and which, he feared, would prevent him addressing them. He told what he had done in other countries; what he had done in America. I cannot say that his manner warmed: but it became more deeply earnest—almost painfully so. He compared his labours to those of St. Paul; and spoke of himself as of an apostle sent, expressly, to preach temperance, on the value of which and on the evils of the contrary vice, he, of course, enlarged. He regretted that his ill-health would not permit him to speak longer; but he had caught it while labouring in the cause, and, therefore, would he glory in his infirmity.

All this was very painful. It was painful to see the labouring of that heaving chest—almost the throbbing of that apparently-overcharged brain; and to hear the words so slowly enunciated, yet with that fearful earnestness, I expected to see him every moment smitten where he stood, and fall in another fit. But he concluded without accident; inviting those who wished to take the pledge to come forward to the rails at the foot of the altar. There was then a rush!—a crowd-rush of whom three-fourths were females. Women, hard working women, half of whom had babies in their arms, knelt down and repeated the oath for themselves and their babies: boys and girls of all ages pushed forward and took the pledge. Many, very many men, also took it. I know not the number; but very many hundreds must have bound themselves that day. I forget the wording of the pledge. I did not like it: it was a most solemn promise uttered by Father Mathew and repeated by each one: then he signed the cross over each, exclaiming: " Carry this sign of the cross unstained by any breach of the pledge, until we meet again at the great judgment seat of God."

There has always been a difference of opinion amongst the Catholic clergy of all countries in which the pledge has been administered, as to the light in which it ought to be considered. Though asserted not to be an oath, and that it might be broken without sin, it was delivered and impressed upon the people in a manner suited only to the most solemn oath. And though declared to be only a promise, yet was the breach of it declared to be a " reserved case" in Ireland. It was not an oath, but the people, in fact, took it as if it were one : and children and babies, men and women, even in a state of maudlin intoxication and unknowing what they did, were permitted to pledge themselves in a manner which those even who administered the ceremonial could hardly define or understand.

" Now, Paddy, my good friend," said an American Catholic bishop to an emigrant who was about to take the pledge ; " will you understand what it is you are going to do ! You are going to make a solemn promise to God, and you ought not to break your promise : but it is a promise, it is not an oath ; understand that it is not an oath."

"Oh no, your reverence," replied Paddy; "sure I understand that it is ten million times more binding nor any oath."

After the ceremonial, hundreds rushed to the secretary to buy temperance medals.

The authoress of that clever caricature entitled "The Domestic Manners of the Americans," or, as the Americans said it ought to have been worded, "Manners of the American Domestics," had raised a fantastic building at Cincinnati, which still went by the name of "Trollope's Folly." In it, she was said to have opened a store of millinery; but as her stock came from London, the fashions were too antiquated for ladies who had theirs direct from Paris; and the speculation did not succeed. I had already seen enough of American women to be quite aware that nothing but the most rapid communication between the scene of their display and the armoury whence they draw their charms, could satisfy their vain longings, or the longings of their vanity, for dress. The store is now, therefore, applied to other purposes.

I was waked one night at Cincinnati—or,

as the inhabitants please to pronounce the name, Cincinnata—by the violent clang of bells rung backwards; and, going to the window, I saw a glorious blaze amongst the buildings at no great distance. The lurid flames and sparks were flying upwards and casting a ruddy glow on the steeples and hills around. Knowing that the throng of people to a fire is always a great hindrance to the efforts of the firemen, I watched the flames from my window for some little time, and then philosophically returned to bed again. I drove past the scene of the disaster on the following day, and saw the blackened remains of a large hog-slaughter-house and packing establishment. I was told that the fire was probably the work of the proprietor, who, wishing to enlarge his establishment, had burnt down the old one after insuring it. All buildings are erected here, not only according to the means of the person for whom they are built, but on a calculation of the time in which, according to the average of cases, he will have made his fortune, and will want to enlarge his premises. That time arrived, in the course of five, ten, or fifteen

CHAP. VIII.—THE PLEDGE.

years, he ensures and burns down his more modest store, and runs up another large enough to hold him for a few years more, when that also follows its predecessors, and makes way for something better.

The fillet inside the loins of pork does not salt or pack profitably. I know not why. The most choice and delicate fillets are, therefore, to be bought here fresh, at one cent, or one halfpenny, a pound.

A propos to eating: I was surprised to hear that the governing authorities of Cincinnati forbid the sale of fish during certain seasons, the food being then thought to be injurious to the public health. Most of the fish from the great lakes is said to be very debilitating. I saw sometimes offered for sale, in the market, some most extraordinary-looking animals out of the Ohio river. They were not like any fish that I had ever seen in Europe: certainly, according to an American saying, when the Almighty created turbot, soles, salmon, and others of that description, the devil must have let these Ohio monsters slip through his fingers.

The Jesuits have a large establishment at

Cincinnati. St. Xavier's College is under their direction, and gives education in the classics, modern languages, chemistry, and natural history, to about two hundred and fifty students, including boarders and day-scholars. I heard a very good account of the establishment, though I had afterwards reason to believe that the influx of day-scholars of every religion and class in the town, and whose numbers equal those of the regular boarders, acts prejudicially upon the Catholic youth, who would wish to pursue their education more steadily and quietly. But in this country, the education of all the first classes of Protestants seems to be entrusted to the Catholic priests and nuns. The lads are sent to Jesuit and other colleges: the girls to convents. The parents say that their children are better taught and better looked after than they would be in any other schools: the teachers say that they do not interfere with the religious opinions of the non-Catholic pupils; and that, without such indiscriminate admission of all, they would not be able to support their establishments. Three-fourths of the boarders in many convents are Protestants.

The Protestant parents who gave me these accounts of the mode in which their children were being educated, generally interrupted the conversation to laugh at the English parliament, which was then expending a whole session in passing what it called the "Ecclesiastical Titles' Bill"—as if, said the Americans, it could matter to the state by what unrecognised names any number of citizens pleased to call themselves! The creation of a Cardinal Archbishop, they said, was a compliment to England, as they themselves were well pleased that Bishop Purcell had just been made archbishop of Cincinnati; and they were inclined to join with American Catholics in considering that Rome slighted their country by not giving them an American cardinal. Thus, while the Prime Minister and the legislature of England were lashing themselves into a fury about clerical puerilities, the civilized and half-civilized world stood by laughing!

But this good feeling is maintained, not only by the absence of all political supremacy, but also by the prudence of the different religionists. Thus at a convocation or council of the Catholic hierarchy, at St. Louis, it had recently been proposed, by the French bishops there, to enforce upon all the Catholic clergy of the United States, the wearing of the straight Roman collar, and of a distinctive clerical habit, instead of the common black dress which they now wear; after much discussion, some of the American-born bishops had said, " Decide what you please; but we know the feelings of our countrymen; and we will not mark out our clergy and make them objects of distrust by giving them a dress different from the usual clerical dress of the country,—a distinction which we know would be considered an assumption, and excite jealousy or dislike; whatever, therefore, you decree, we shall enjoin upon our own clergy to continue to dress themselves as much like gentlemen as possible; though always in black." In consequence of such determined remonstrance, no decree was made.

Had such prudent counsels prevailed in England, no act would have been thought of to forbid people from dressing in the habit of their order; or, in other words, from wearing their own clothes; for nothing in the act now prevents the Passionist, Father Spencer, from wearing the habit of the Carthusian Abbot Burdon! Well may the world laugh at the puerilities of English ecclesiastical legislation!

Not being able to hire any residence in the town of Cincinnati, I enquired about the many mineral springs in the neighbourhood, which are, more or less, places of fashionable resort; but as places of fashionable resort they seemed alone to be considered; for the first medical practitioner in the town could give me little information as to the quality of their waters; and, to my enquiry whether any of them contained iron, he said he " guessed not; but if not, it was easy to add it."

Private letters and the public papers, however, now informed me that the cholera was dying away at St. Louis, while it seemed to be increasing at Cincinnati; and we prepared to push onwards on our journey. Again, we attempted to hire servants, used to the country; and a nice tidy Irish girl was recommended to us. Her mother and she had lately emigrated, and had spent most of their little money in bringing so far the feather beds they had prized in Ireland, while the friends they had expected to meet had died in Cincinnati before their arrival. My wife was much pleased with their manners, and gladly hired the girl; but here again the engagement came to nought. On the day on which we were to start, the mother could not bring herself to part with her daughter, and the daughter could not go with us against the mother's wishes. At Cincinnati, therefore, they remained; adding to the number of the Irish emigrants who almost starve one another on its wharves. I tried to persuade some of the porters and carmen how much better they would prosper farther up the country; but sure there was Mary and the children were hard to move; and sure they had spent all their money; and when they did earn a dollar, the whiskey was very comforting, and three cents would roll a man in the gutter, and make him good for nothing at all, at all.

Well might Father Mathew preach temperance to such people. The more settled population of the country, however, needed him not; for before his arrival, the walls had been covered with handbills in favour of what was called the Maine Liquor Law, which forbids the selling, by retail, of all spirituous and fermented liquor. The votes were shortly afterwards taken on the question by universal suffrage; and by an immense majority of votes, the whole people of the state of Ohio (a territory more than half as large as all France), imposed upon themselves this vexatious, tyrannous, absurd sumptuary law!

We paid our bill, one dollar a-head per day for board, lodging, and service; found one Irish hackney coach driver, who consented to convey our children half a quarter of a mile to the quay for half a dollar; three others having turned away in disgust at my meanness in having offered only a little more than double the London fare. We crossed the busy quay, and embarked ourselves and our goods on "the river of beautiful waters," the bright Ohio.

CHAPTER IX.

THE OHIO.

Rivers of England and of America.—Kentucky or Ohio; freedom or slavery.—Plan for emancipation of slaves.—La Belle Rivière.—Vineyards.—Cholera.—Maddison.—The Mammoth Cave.—Aspect of Indiana.

AT this time, a story was going the round of the American papers, recounting that a Britisher, who, in a railway carriage in Europe, was dilating to an American on the greatness of England, exclaimed, " Yes, sir, the Thames is a magnificent river: it is one of the finest rivers in the world. It is navigable for nearly one hundred miles!"

" In my country," responded the American, " there is a river, called the Ohio, which is navigable for one thousand miles, until it joins two other rivers, one of which has been navigable for one thousand, and the other for eighteen hundred, miles; and from whence all three flow together for more than one thousand miles more to the sea. The Britisher," continues the American who told the story, " did not say anything ; but he looked at me with an air of offended dignity, to make me understand that I ought not to have insulted such an one as him by trying to impose fables upon him ; and he then majestically went from my side to the furthest seat in the carriage."

We were now embarked upon the first of these three rivers, which, formed at Pittsburgh by the junction of two others, that had been severally navigable to keel boats for about two hundred and fifty miles, had thence been called the Ohio, and had already carried down our steamboat five hundred miles to us at Cincinnati. I remember, some years ago, reading an account of the seizure of a vessel in some European port, as with forged papers, for pretending that she came from a place called Pittsburgh : and it was with difficulty the people who had seized her could be persuaded that a little village had arisen three thousand miles from any sea, where this vessel had been built, and whence it had sailed across the Atlantic.

However, the Ohio had now left the busy

town of Pittsburgh five hundred miles behind; and here it was at Cincinnati, and here we were upon it.

From what is called the *Levee* or floating wharf, which rises and falls with the river, we had easily stepped, from the paved shore or bank at Cincinnati, on board the St. Louis mail-packet, on which we now settled ourselves. We passed the four steam-ferries which constantly unite the city with its suburbs on the opposite side; we passed the city itself; and soon lost sight even of its beautifully-situated observatory: we swept round from amongst the crowd of steamers and flat boats that surrounded us, and soon found ourselves in comparative solitude on the smooth bosom of this lovely river. On both sides, the scenery was broken, diversified, and beautiful. Sometimes that of Kentucky was the most picturesque; sometimes that of Ohio State most delighted us. And as some of my family already revolted against the free and levelling manners of the Free States, and wished that their location should be in a slave state, where they would meet with more of the deference to which they had been accustomed, a friendly contest was kept up amongst us as the scenery on the Ohio or the Kentucky shore was, in turn, the most beautiful.

"Look there!" one of them would cry, "look at those beautiful woods, look at that beautiful secluded glen on the left! What a sweet, quiet, gentlemanly location, as they call it, one might have there!"

"In the backwoods, indeed!" one, of the opposite faction amongst us, would exclaim. "Why, nothing living is in sight there! Look at the pretty cultivated country in free Ohio. Look at the churches and farmhouses, and... yes, look at the vines on those terraces sloping down to the river. See how far a-head the free state is of the slave state!"

Thus, in friendly contest, the hours and the miles past by us; the broad stream winding slowly, now to the right and now to the left, amid those beautiful forests or cultivated bluffs. And whatever might be the cause of the difference, the youngest child in my party could not but contrast the busy cultivation, mills and factories on the one side, with the beautiful but silent forest on the Kentucky shore of the river. And whereas I had already found out that land on the Ohio side could not be purchased for less than from one to two hundred dollars an acre, I had been offered, and was now again offered thousands of acres on the Kentucky shore at twenty-five cents or one shilling an acre. I may be told that inferiority and barrenness of the soil occasioned the difference : no soil could be worse than that of the busiest scenes through which we had passed on the railway from Albany: and here, on the banks of the Ohio, on the shores of a water carriage of five thousand miles, one would suppose any location to be valuable.

I would not enter into the question of domestic slavery in the United States. Let the free soilers, let the free states and the slave states discuss the matter amongst themselves according to their own prudence. I am convinced that a great deal of harm has been done and is still being done to the cause of freedom by the officious intrusion of foreigners into the question. Least of all should the English, whose ancestors introduced the curse into these countries, whose laws upheld and defended it, least of all should they pharisaically reproach the North Americans with the institution. Let us not be told that the English grew ashamed of the iniquity and abolished it in their own colonies. How many years ago did they do so? Is the power so to boast fifteen or twenty years old? And how did they abolish it? Did their love of justice prompt them to come forward frankly and at once, saying: " We will ransom these captives from their masters:" or were not Lord Stanley and the ministry obliged to draw them on gradually, by first asking for a loan of twenty millions, which, when the philanthropic mind was prepared for some sacrifice, they converted into a gift of twenty millions to the West Indian planters? Would they have taxed themselves to the amount of twenty millions, if it had first been proposed? I doubt it.

But, the deed is done: we have bought up these captives: some twenty or fifteen years ago, we did tax ourselves and our descendants to perform a great act of justice to the slaves —perhaps of injustice to their owners. But are the circumstances of England and of the West Indies at all similar to those of one of the slave states of America? I say of one of the slave states: for understand, if you can, that each state is independent in its legislature, and can no more coerce another state than you can coerce France. England, wealthy England, in its united empire, could buy off the slaves of a distant colony: and, therefore, it argues that Kentucky, with its population of only seven hundred thousand free whites, can ransom its two hundred thousand domestic slaves. How many ounces of slave property did each British subject pay for? How many ounces of slave flesh did we pay for per head? Was it a cognizable fraction of an ounce? And yet we insult poor Kentucky because each one of its free citizens is not prepared to ransom one quarter of a slave for his own share! Our British enthusiasts are fond of quoting Shylock and talking about "the pound of flesh": let them here work out the calculation they are so fond of.

Let me not be misunderstood. I am no apologist for slavery. I loathe the system. My soul recoils from and denounces it in every, the most mitigated shape. I would only withhold our own well-meaning but ignorant friends of the negro, from rushing blindly into the difficulties, and embittering the feelings of those whose position they do not understand. None know the evils of slavery better than the owners of slaves ; better than the owners of land in the slave states of America. None know better than they that slave labour is dearer than free labour would be if they could obtain it : none know better than they that slavery prevents the tide of free labour from setting towards them :—that, where all labourers are slaves, the poorest Irishman will not go where he would sink to a par with slaves : none know better than the owners of land in these States, that emigrants from Europe avoid them, and that, consequently, their property has no value compared to that of which European competition enhances the price. None know better than they that the evil must go on increasing ; and that the slave states, that border upon the free states, must be daily impoverished by the superior attractions of the latter; and that no " compromise", however rigidly enforced, will avert the comparative bankruptcy that ultimately awaits them. They know that slavery is the curse of their country; but they know that they received the legacy from England, and they despair of ever getting rid of it.

Every census tells them that while the free population of Pennsylvania, which contains forty-four millions of square miles, has quadrupled itself during the present century, and that while that of New York which contains forty-six millions of square miles has increased more than five-fold, the free population of the neighbouring slave states of Virginia and of North Carolina, each of which also contains forty-four millions of square miles, has not even doubled itself; that the united population of these two first mentioned states in 1850 was more than five millions three hundred thousand; and that that of the other two states, containing, be it remembered, nearly the same average, scarcely amounted to one million three hundred thousand. Is it to be supposed that slave owners and landed proprietors in slave states do not meditate upon such facts as these? Is it to be supposed that they do not remember that, while the free population in Pennsylvania and New York has thus wonderfully increased, that of the slaves in these states has been allowed to die off, and has been quite extinguished?—and that while the free population of Virginia and North Carolina has been, comparatively speaking, stationary, the number of the slaves in those two states has almost doubled itself, and is now within one-third of that of the whites? Is it to be supposed that land proprietors and slave owners are blind to these facts, are incapable of tracing effects to their causes? They must foresee the bankruptcy that awaits them. They must be aware that slavery is the curse of their country; but, again I say, they know that they received the legacy from England, and they despair of ever getting rid of it.

In self-defence, they will be obliged to do so. As a well-wisher to them and to the slaves, whom I would believe they unwillingly hold in bondage, may I be permitted to suggest to them a plan for effecting the object that all good men must have at heart?

The evil already existing, two things must be borne in mind by practical abolitionists who would preserve the slave owners from ruin, and the country from desolation. It is useless to ask the owners in a body to liberate their slaves without compensation; to forego, without compensation, the property which, rightly or wrongly, they possess. Were they suddenly to do so, the slaves would probably refuse to work; starvation, pillage, and murder would ensue. It is necessary therefore to find:

Firstly, Compensation to the owner.

Secondly, Free labour to supply the place of the slave labour that shall have been withdrawn.

Let us assume the labour of a male slave to be worth to his owner, one dollar and forty cents a-day; (double or halve my figures as you will; I only wish to state a principle); and that he works for fourteen hours out of the twenty-four; each hour, therefore, will be worth ten cents. Say that there are twenty-eight working days in the month; why not declare that every slave shall have power to ransom the last working hour of every working day in some one month in the year, on payment to his owner of twenty-eight times ten cents, or two dollars and eighty cents? If the slaves have not the means, I am sure that I am not rating too high the patriotism and kind feeling of their owners, when I say that they would make them a present of this one hour in one month of the year to start them on their way to emancipation. With what they might earn during this first one hour, they would in time be able to redeem another last hour in another month of the year; and so on until the last hour of every day in every month, and, by degrees, the last two hours and the last three hours, and, last blessed hope of all! every hour of every month were thus gradually redeemed!

Suppose the plan to be carried out, what habits of industry would be engendered in the slaves! What hopes would excite the toil of those who wished for freedom! Many there are who wish for it not, and these might remain as they are, if they strove not to redeem their servitude. Meanwhile, the proprietor would be receiving the full value for his slave, and would have time to make his arrangements to supply the place of the emancipated ones as they individually acquired their freedom in the order of their industry.

I am quite aware that the scheme may be laughed at: that I may be told that I am proposing to pay the slave owner about eighty dollars for a month's freedom, or nine hundred dollars for the whole freedom of a slave. As I have said, I care not for the figures; alter them as you will: I merely suggest a principle to the "men of good will" among the slave owners. If they have this good will which I impute to them, they will easily devise public offices in which the value of each slave may be recorded; in which each slave may register the hours that shall have been redeemed; in which each slave may bequeath the hours he shall have so redeemed to any other slave; so that, in case of death while working out his freedom, the toil may not be lost to his family or race. All these are details which those who are willing may easily arrange. And, in the meanwhile, were all slave owners, in these transition states, to agree to clothe their slaves in a particular uniform which should mark them as such, those slaves who first work out their freedom would not have to prove it by removing to a Free State, and emigrants would not be deterred from settling amongst them by the fear of being confounded with slave labourers.

Such, then, is an outline of the plan for emancipation which I would submit to the slave owners of the United States. I impute not to them the evil at which humanity sickens. Still less do I presume to dictate. Apart from the eternal principles of justice, apart from the everlasting sentiment of right and wrong which the whole human race feels to be insulted by their institutions—it is their own affair and that of their slaves. But by that everlasting sentiment of right and wrong, but by those eternal principles of justice, but by their wish to improve the morality and to perfect the civilisation of some of the most beautiful portions of the globe, I call upon them, I BESEECH THEM TO DO SOMETHING.

Our steamer still moved onwards adown the

beautiful Ohio. About sixteen miles below Cincinnati, we had admired the situation of the house in which the late General Harrison, President of the United States, had resided, and where was now his grave: we had admired the locality and floated by it, little thinking in how short a time the grandson of him who lay buried there would be bound up in all our sorrows, would be a mainstay and a solace in the despair that was to overwhelm us. We chatted thoughtlessly of the history of the late President and of the pretty country around his last home. We thought that we could have nothing in common with the statesman buried on the banks of the Ohio, and we floated gaily by.

We soon passed the boundary of Ohio State, and wound along beside that Indiana of which I have recorded that I had so long thought with interest, as the future home of some of my boys; the home which I had long wished to explore in dreams and visions—though feeling, all the while, how visionary was the wish. And yet, here I was with all my children around me: here, on the western side of the broad Atlantic; in the centre of the wide continent of North America: far beyond what all England considers the utmost boundary of the slight civilization of a half-civilized land! Here I was with my wife and eleven children, speeding down the great Ohio river, between the dark pine forests of Kentucky and the oak-clearings of Indiana. . . . I felt, indeed, as a friend had told me at Cincinnati, that I was either a hero or a madman!

The average width of the Ohio, during its course of one thousand and fifteen miles, is said to be about half a mile. It did not look to us anything like so wide, either because, from our recent acquaintance with American scenery,

" Our minds had grown colossal",

or because, the waters being low, much of its bed was now laid dry. For between March and September, these waters generally rise and fall a matter of fifty feet: they often rise twelve feet in a single night. During the winter half of the year, first-class steamboats navigate its whole course: during the summer, these are gradually exchanged for smaller ones, which draw the least possible water: and even these so often run aground, that the passage may then be almost said to be entirely impeded. At this time, we had no danger of being delayed; though rushes and flags grew up from the bottom and floated on a great part of the surface of the water. I can scarcely imagine the appropriateness of the name, La belle Rivière, when it was first given to the stream by the French. At that time, and until it was kept constantly ploughed and harrowed and tossed about by the paddles of almost innumerable steamboats, the whole face of the river was covered with rushes and weeds, that made it as green as any meadow. In fact, it has no current to wash these away: its waters never flow faster than three miles an hour, not even in March, when they are highest; and, in the summer season, they do not advance more than one mile in the hour. Add to this that the descent is uniform during the whole of its length, being about five inches in the mile; that there are no rapids, no falls, except one small descent at Louisville, which disappears when the waters are high. Lazily, therefore, the broad stream pursues its winding course amid beautifully-wooded banks and precipitous cliffs, formed by the wash of the waters through the alluvial soil of the mighty valley that lies between the Alleghany mountains and the table land that bounds the great lakes on the northward. They are hills and cliffs to those floating down the river; but they are only beautiful ravines and breaks in the table land of the valley, to those who stand on the top of them.

It was a pleasant voyage we enjoyed down the Ohio in this St. Louis mail steampacket. We passed the pretty scenery on each side at the rate of about fourteen miles an hour. We stopped often for official or commercial purposes—to deliver letters or to take in goods. No wharves or quays were prepared at the different points of landing; but old, worn-out steamboats, from which the machinery had been removed, were moored to the banks, and, rising and falling with the increase or lessening of the waters, formed excellent floating piers. We passed the village of Vevay, in Switzerland county, in the centre of its pretty vineyards planted on terraces sloping from the summit of the cliffs to the edge of the water. This place had been settled, about forty years before, by some thirty Swiss families to whom the United States had sold the land a bargain, that they might introduce the cultivation of the vine into the country. They did so; and have since been joined by many of their countrymen from Europe. Vines are little grown in North America. They require a more continuous care, and, above all, they give a slower return for money first invested, than suits the habits of the people : but when cultivated in an exposition that agrees with them, the result is very satisfactory. But commerce unshackled knows best how to employ its capital. I have drunk native-grown wine of such excellence at Cincinnati, that assuredly Americans would be guilty of folly in sending for the Champagne *tisanne* and light wines of France and of the Rhine, when they can produce better on their own soil, inasmuch as their summers are hotter, did not commercial experience tell them that their capital and

CHAP. IX.—THE OHIO. 247

energies can be more profitably employed than in the cultivation of the vine.

The Kentucky river flows into the Ohio nearly opposite Vevay. It seems to be a beautiful stream, with a very rapid current, between high precipitous banks of rock. It is navigable to small boats for about one hundred and fifty miles; and at a place called Frankfort, a net-work of railways to the interior begins.

We had dined on board our steamer, and were now approaching the end of our pleasant voyage. I would gladly have gone down the Ohio to a town called Cairo, where it flows into the Mississippi, and have thence ascended the latter stream to St. Louis: but cholera still prevailed on the shore and in the boats of the Mississippi; and the ship fever, brought up from New Orleans at this time of the year, was said to linger about many of them. We had, therefore, resolved to land on the right bank of the river and find our way, as best we might, across the states of Indiana and Illinois. About six o'clock in the afternoon, our steamer drew nigh to the landing at Maddison, an important place in Indiana, ninety-two miles from Cincinnati — a distance which we had passed over in seven hours, at a cost of one and a half dollar for each grown-up person, including dinner.

Our children and the diminished number of our pets, polly and the canary birds, were quickly transferred to the disabled steamer that served the purpose of a floating wharf. Our baggage was hauled upon it and covered its crazy deck. Amongst this, was a guitar which the porter of the hotel caught hold of; and casting his eyes around at the unusually large party and at the baggage, imperials and carriage-boxes of shapes such as he had never before seen, paused a moment in meditation as to what we could be. He was a native American. Emigrants are fair game to such; and, after a while, he exclaimed, whether in jest or earnest, I know not,

"Oh, then you are the company that has leased the concert house! When do you open it?"

"To-night," I replied: "and you shall be my first fiddle, in a cap and bells."

The people, who had congregated around, laughed at the retort: and we all proceeded in good humour to the hotel.

Maddison is said to be a very thriving place. It did not appear so to me: but rather declining or stationary. And, indeed, referring to the census of the United States, I find that the population of its county is entered in the year 1840 as having been 9,025, while in 1850 it was only 10,031. This is corroborative of my recollection of its state of decay: an increase of ten per cent. in ten years is tantamount to a decrease in this country. Why the very next county in alphabetical order in my little book, is thus entered:—" Mahoning, 1840, none: 1850, 23,745—increase, 23,745"! That is what we call here being alive!

I should have been very glad to have made an incursion into Kentucky to visit its MAMMOTH CAVE, had not the cholera and the heat of the weather made us dread delay. The cave, it is true, has not been explored more than a distance of about twenty miles, which are supposed to be only a beginning of its subterraneous ramifications: but a cavern twenty miles under ground, which contains, as this is said to contain, two hundred and twenty-six avenues, forty-seven domes, many rivers, and eight cataracts, would appear rather extensive to a mere British stranger. I should have liked to see the underground natural "church", big enough to contain five thousand sittings; the " haunted room" in which the two Indian mummies were found; "Goram's dome", six hundred and twenty feet high; and the "bottomless pit", into which visitors are let down by cords tied round their waists. I should have gladly seen the walls and roofs of polished stalactites, and the floors covered with sulphate of lime as white as snow and sparkling like diamonds:—to have taken boat in the underground river and have floated to the "rocky mountains", as they term a vast ridge of stalactites in one of these immense halls. But as several days would have been required to investigate this wondrous cavern, and as the beautiful scenery around it would doubtless have seduced us still further from our route, we resisted temptation; and talked of the puny caverns of Matlock and of Torquay, to prove that we already knew what the inside of the world was like. We resisted temptation, and turned our backs on green Kentucky.

I did not like Maddison. I heard that cholera was in the town: and the hotel, the Maddison House, was uncomfortable and exorbitant in its charges. I noted it in my memorandum book as to be avoided:—a rather amusing caution on the part of one who was not very likely to travel that road again during the present conformation of this globe and universe! We slept here one night; and, on the following morning, at seven o'clock, took our seats in the railway cars for Indianapolis. I had had much discussion in the office to induce them to take my luggage, which they insisted ought to follow by a goods train, as there was some wonderful hill to be ascended, and great weight would be trying to the engine. However, the matter was settled at last in consideration of four and a half dollars being paid for extra luggage.

After leaving Maddison, we soon came to this hill up the banks of the Ohio to the table land above. It was a very steep inclined plane—steeper than any I have seen in England or Wales; but a magnificent engine, made in England, drew us slowly to the top. We then passed through a country that was very pleasing. Forests of oak and beech trees covered the land; except where, here and there, they had been removed from some small clearing, some farmhouse, village or rising town. The cars rattled through many of these, in the very streets of which the stumps of the recent forest yet stood, two or three feet above ground, and obliged all wayfarers to turn aside. Hence the origin of the American expression " to be stumped." The busy community had not yet had time to dig them up. This would be done when they were more settled. Through the shady woods (it was a hot day in June), through the shady woods, beautiful cool ravines opened into the boundless forest: adown them, leapt and sparkled bright rivulets that ought to have harboured delicious trout. I was told that they contained no fish; as the waters quite disappear during the summer months. This scenery was much more pleasing than that we had heretofore passed through; inasmuch as beech, oak and other trees had replaced the monotonous Scotch firs of New York and the north of Ohio States; and, when they occasionally opened and showed us small prairies and park-like grounds, I fancied how pleasant a backwoodsman's life would be in such a scenery, in such a sunny climate. We were determined to be pleased with Indiana; and already discovered that the manners of the " Hoosiers," as its inhabitants are familiarly called, were much more gentle and considerate than those of the go-a-head " Buckeys" of Ohio State. I had much pleasant and instructive talk with one or two persons in the cars; and we were, altogether, highly gratified by this very decided advance towards the Far West, the backwoods and the prairies of North America.

At two o'clock, we arrived at Indianapolis, the capital of the state. We had come a distance of eighty-six miles in seven hours;— slow work, but the inclined plane had delayed us. We had paid two dollars and a half per grown up person for our places, which perhaps was rather dear. But the cars were perfectly comfortable: the managers and people had been very attentive and obliging: and, in short, we had had a very pleasant ride.

CHAPTER X.

INDIANAPOLIS.

Hotel at Indianapolis.—Punkahs.—Manners of Americans.—
A "gone 'coon."—Difficulty of going further.—An isolated
priest.—Colonel and Mrs. Drake.—Plan of American cities.—
A morning visit.—A spirit shop.—The Capitol.—Walks.—
Buying horses.—Buying a wagon.—A carpenter.—American
English.—Buying a location.—The Indiana Sentinel.—American newspapers.—Fashionable shops.

Mr. Turtle, the proprietor or manager of the Wright's House hotel at Indianapolis, seemed to think his premises already too full to accommodate my party; but he showed me a wing of the house, running back between yards and gardens, which I could have if the apartment would suit me. There were several bedrooms, side by side, all communicating with an open balcony and trellis-wood shaded by roses and jasmines in full bloom. We were seduced by the freshness of the flowers; and engaged the rooms at once by the week. We did not consider that, there being no second story over that wing of the house, the sun would strike through the tiles and roof, and raise the temperature of our rooms to that of a moderately-heated oven. When we discovered this to be the case, it was too late to change: and we comforted ourselves by opening the doors upon the flowery balcony and the windows opposite: we so secured a current of air—heated but refreshing.

We went down to dinner in a large room on the ground floor. There were not above a dozen other persons at table; so that we constituted half the company. Here we first saw in use what, in the East Indies, were called "punkas":—above the whole length of the dinner table, several light frameworks of wood, covered with paper, were swung upon hinges from the ceiling, and hung down within a couple of feet of the tablecloth: a cord passed through and was knotted to the bottom of each framework, and was then carried on through pullies to the further side of the room. This a negro waiter boy was pulling steadily, and so caused the hanging screens to wave backwards and forwards above the table; thus not only a delicious current of air was kept up, but, also, the flies were dispersed that congregated, in black patches, upon the dishes whenever the lad paused to rest in his monotonous exercise. It was a most simple and inexpensive, but a most delightful way of being fanned.

The company consisted of either boarders in the house or travellers. They were all quite inoffensive. Indeed all Americans are so at their meals. As they grudge every minute which they steal from business for the purposes of eating, and as they never, or scarcely ever drink wine, beer or spirits, they have every motive to be silent and none to talk. Although they, of course, want the polish of the highest circles, their manners are very much better than those of the same class in England: and, indeed, their universal politeness to women is unequalled, unapproached even by any class in any country. Here are no fussy *petits soins* and fidgeting complimentary interference, such as Sterne finds so delightful: but a show of genuine respect for a petticoat by whomsoever worn. In no saloon, in no steamboat throughout the United States, will any man, of whatsoever rank, retain a seat while any woman of whatsoever rank is standing without one. Like Byron, they

"reverence a petticoat:
A garment of a mystical sublimity,
Whether it be of muslin, silk, or dimity."

But though the Americans do not drink wine or beer at these *tables d'hôte*, they are not sparing of iced water, the one universal luxury. Here, also, for the first time, we saw tea drunk at dinner: large boilers full of tea were standing on a side table, and the women especially were frequent applicants for it. I tried the mixture; and can truly recommend a large bowl of strong tea, with a large lump of ice floating and quickly melting in the middle of it, as being most palatable,—at a midday dinner during the dog days.

But now I found that I was fairly stumped; I was done for; I was a gone 'coon. Having told the reader the meaning of the former expression, I may as well here remark the derivation of the latter phrase, which I now often heard around me. It seems that some celebrated sportsman, some American Colonel

Hawker, being out with his gun that was never known to miss its aim, espied a racoon in a tree and levelled his piece.

" Don't give yourself the trouble, Colonel Hawker;" said the poor animal. " I know my fate. You never miss. Don't trouble yourself to fire. I conclude to come down to you. I am a gone 'coon."

My situation at Indianapolis, I found to be about as helpless as that of the 'coon. I had come by steamboat and railway as far as railway or steamboat could forward me in this direction. Water there was no more of; and the railways were completed no further. It was true that several lines were planned out, which would go to St. Louis and the Pacific: but we had no wish to stay at Indianapolis until they should be completed. I had been told that the stage-coach, direct from Cincinnati, passed through the town and along the National Road to the Mississippi: and to this I had trusted. The stage coach came rolling up the street.

I will not describe what has been described so often: suffice it to say that the one body of the vehicle held places for three with their backs to the horses; and places for three with their faces to the horses; and a bench across, from door to door, for three more, the only support for whose shoulders was a leathern strap drawn across from end to end. These were only nine places, even could they be all secured, which was doubtful: and nine places would not suffice to my party. Moreover, the coach started in the evening, and we should have to travel all that and the following night. It was not to be thought of. What could be done! I was a gone 'coon!"

"Not at all," said Mr. Turtle: "do as we all do. Buy a wagon and a pair of horses, and drive across the prairie."

The spirit of adventure was upon us; and the idea was rather taking.

We walked out to evening service. It was the festival of Corpus Christi: and we called upon the priest. Poor, Reverend Mr. Guéguen, he was in a desponding state! We were no longer in the go-a-head diocese of Cincinnati; but in the old diocese of Vincennes, founded by the French settlers of Louisiana, where French clergy and the apathy of French routine have to contend with American energy. Four bare brick walls were, indeed, roofed in for a church : but whitewash and plaster there was not ; pavement to the floor there was not. There was a capital organ, but no one to play on it or to sing. Mr. Guéguen, himself of French origin, had been there for many years: he had himself created whatever now existed ; but he seemed to despair of doing any more. He himself was living, apparently broken-hearted, in poverty and dirt and the noise of the dozen children of the Irishman with whom he boarded. The town, indeed, could boast many handsome churches, handsomely finished for every other denomination of Christians : but the members of government and of the legislature met at Indianapolis, as it was the capital of the State ; and the clergy of the several denominations called upon all to subscribe to their several funds. He had not the spirit to do this. When the clergy of all other denominations administered the Lord's Supper in their churches, they sent round invitation cards amongst themselves, and they all paid one another the compliment of attending and partaking, in their several temples, in turn: this kept up a bond of good fellowship—a liberal kind of " Communion of Saints"—in which a Catholic priest could not join. Poor Mr. Guéguen! he did not say all this to me. Though he preached an excellent sermon, he was a small talker: but I found out that such was his position relatively to the others.

He introduced us to the great lady of his congregation, an Irishwoman by birth, married to Colonel Drake. The colonel was a thorough American; and I saw a good deal of him with encreasing pleasure. There is so much freshness in the style of conversation, so much playful energy in the expressions of these children of a fresh new world! A literary friend, whom I should be proud to name, said to me in London: " The Americans have a very disagreeable way of talking through their noses: and yet, when any one of them is speaking at my table, I am very sorry if an Englishman interrupts him: I learn something new from the American." Colonel Drake was, I think, treasurer for the State; and seemed to be a popular man and well spoken of by all. I went to his little office where his two clerks were writing:—seated, indeed, but with the left leg of each resting upon the desk beside the inkstand: the right leg of one of them was tumbling about a stool behind him. The gallant colonel was swinging himself upon three or four chairs at once, smoking and spitting out of the open window. There must be something very attractive in these attitudes; for I own that, by this time, I and all my boys were as fond of balancing ourselves upon two or three chairs as any American of them all: and my girls loved the rocking chairs and fans.

Colonel Drake highly approved of the plan of travelling that had been recommended to me. He knew all that country and most of the Far West; having formerly farmed and dealt largely in horses beyond the Mississippi. He himself, I found, had a pair of horses that he would sell; and though he did not press them upon me, he offered to show them. I got into his rough-and-ready, and he drove me to his house.

We passed from the main street of the town,

which is of handsome width, with broad pavements on each side, and across two or three other streets diverging from it at right angles, and which, as far as they went, gave, also, promise of being handsome. But vacancies soon appeared between the houses in the lines in which these are, hereafter, to be completed; and more and more garden ground was enclosed around each, until it should be needed to be built upon. This seems to be the method followed in all these American towns. The plan having been first laid out and the boundaries of the township being defined, buildings diverge from the core, and, here and there, dot the line of the future streets, until they lose themselves in the forest, the prairie, or the cultivated land. As the vacancies on each side of the streets are filled up, side pavements are made, trees are planted to overshadow them, the centre of the street is paved, and gas and waterpipes are laid down. Thus this city of Indianapolis was, as yet, but one continuous street, with stems of other streets shooting off from it; but the plan of the rising town was definitively settled, and although the boundaries of the township enclosed cultivated and waste land, like the walls of Rome, the scattered buildings already contained a population of ten thousand inhabitants.

The residence of Colonel Drake was beyond the buildings, and stood off on a grassy common bestrewn with giant trees that had been, apparently, cut down for no other reason than that the axeman had a few hours of spare time. It was a very pretty villa, in a gay flower garden, overshadowed by handsome oak trees. The interior was nicely, and even elegantly furnished. We paid our visit to Mrs. Drake, who was a handsome, ladylike woman, and were then shown into another room where a tray was nicely spread with refreshments for us The colonel and I went to look at the horses —a pair of remarkably pretty iron greys— well bred, three years old and about fifteen hands high. I thought them rather too slight and too young for my work; but we harnessed them to the rough-and-ready, and I drove them out for two or three miles. One of them went lame:—a sprain or temporary injury, I believe, of which their owner had not known anything.

But I was fearful of starting on my journey with a lame horse; and I drove back to the villa.

Mrs. Drake had a very large family; the eldest of whom, a nicely-drest girl of twelve years old, was, with her brothers and sisters, playing about the garden and green. None of them wore shoes or stockings.

The colonel himself was a Protestant:—

"It is a great advantage to us, in this country," he said to me, "that Mrs. Drake is a Catholic. We have never been left quite alone."

"How do you mean?" I asked.

"She has never been obliged to cook her own dinner," he explained.

"What can you mean?" I inquired, as much in the dark as before.

"Almost all the helps here, you call them servants," he said, "are Irish Catholic emigrants: and they have that feeling towards Mrs. Drake, as a fellow Catholic, that they have never all left her at once without notice and without any one to do for her. I assure you that she is the only lady in this county who can say as much."

I began to doubt whether it might not be most comfortable to be located in a slave state!

There were two other very good hotels in Indianapolis, the arrivals at which were regularly published in the newspapers! What more could be done in the most fashionable watering place? One of these, opposite to the one we occupied, was called the " Capital House": I expressed surprise at the assumption of the name, which implied that it was the best house in the town ; but was told that it was to have been called the " Capitol House," but that the painter had, by mistake, put an *a* for an *o*, and had not yet had time to alter it : so " Capital House" it continued to be called.

The weather was very hot, and large quantities of iced water used to be drunk in the bar-room of our hotel. This, as usual, was slightly partitioned off from the entrance hall, into which the reading room, well supplied with papers from all parts of America, opened. Spirits were never drunk ; I asked the landlord for a little brandy, and he said he would give me a pint bottle, but dared not sell one : —he charged for it, notwithstanding, in the bill. The law forbidding the retail of intoxicating drink prevailed here. And yet, a few doors from our hotel, a speculator was putting up a spirit shop, which was to be opened when the legislature met. The speculator had calculated that he would be informed against and fined about twenty times during the session; but that his profits would still leave a handsome balance in his favour. I was glad to hear that this absurdly-tyrannical law was thus to be openly defied.

The capitol of Indianapolis—not the capital inn, but the State House—is a remarkably handsome building, of really good classical architecture. It professes to be modelled somewhat after the Parthenon at Athens. The pillars, as well as the rest of the building, are of brick; but stuccoed and painted so well that close examination alone can detect the real material. The churches in the town are also, as I have before observed, more than usually large and well built. Domes, spires, and towers have arisen that would do no discredit to any European capital, and which nobly diversify the large plain in which the city stands. In truth, the situation of the town is excellent—not perhaps as a commercial emporium, since it has no water carriage; but as a residence and the central seat of government. It stands on a high tableland of good soil—dry and healthy: and the streets, as they diverge from the centre, lead to pleasing walks amid farms and forests that my children admired much.

" We used to separate," writes Louie, " into two or three parties and explore the neighbourhood. In one of these walks, we passed a large cherry orchard, where the owner was gathering a beautiful harvest of fruit, which he offered to us liberally. One walk was a particular favourite of mine: I went there first with my eldest brother and sister: it led through a beautiful country, and, after following for some time the course of a little stream, it terminated suddenly at a wood and a neat frame cottage. Large logs of timber lay around; and, as Kenelm wished to explore the forest for a little way, Catharine and I sat down on one of the logs to await his return. A most beautiful bird, of a kind which we had never seen before, soon perched on a tree close to us: but the owner came out of the cottage, accompanied by his two little children, who began playing about, and the bird flew away. Our brother returned with a handful of bright feathers of different colours which he had found in the wood, and a large chrysalis that was, also, new to us."

It was more easy to find perfect seclusion in these country walks, than even in our own rooms:—

"The parrot," Lucy writes, "had made herself widely known by her noise and chattering; and several people, who were staying in the hotel, came to my bedroom, where she was kept, and asked that she should be brought out on the terrace. One day, when I was dressing in my room, some one tried to come in; but, finding the door locked, began knocking authoritatively and crying out 'Open the door, won't you, please!' I did so; and found a woman with a child in her arms who was crying. I asked her what she wanted. Without the slightest apology or word of civility, she replied: 'Where's the bird? I want to show it to baby: he 's so cross, I can't do anything with him! Where 's the bird?'"

Free and easy this!

But unless we wished to take up our abode permanently at Indianapolis, it was necessary that I should procure horses and a wagon, with which to move onwards. I had been put in communication with a man, said to be knowing in horseflesh, who proposed to me to make an excursion into the neighbouring State of Illinois, and there try to pick up some, on their way from the country of the Missouri to the old towns on the eastern seaboard: but I preferred trying what could be done in Indianapolis itself, where the breed of horses, in general use, was excellent. Market days came round; and brought farmers and men of business from a distance of many miles. Here I saw some very fine horses, rather too heavy for me, drawing wagons laden with corn and wheat, which they left at stores and mills, above which was inscribed the usual promise of full cash prices for everything: here were the owners in their buggies or rough-and-readies, or riding beautiful beasts of a stamp rather too light for my work. The horses in the wagons, in the buggies, and even the saddle horses, used to be, all alike, fastened to a paling or a gate in some retired lane in the shade, whence it appeared that any one could loose them and drive or ride off with them miles away into the woods before they should be missed. Their owners had evidently no fear of the kind; and I was assured that the Americans scorned stealing and pilfering. They would overreach, that is to say, they would be extra-sharp in a bargain; but they would not demean themselves to steal.

At length, I was told of a jobber who had a stable full of horses which he would either sell or let to convey me to my destination: and my wife and I continued our walk in the direction of his premises. We were turning into them, when our guide led us into a temperance hotel bar-room, where tea, sherbet and slops were sold, and requested my wife to wait there till our return. Why so? "It was not right for a lady to go to a stable yard"—"People would be shocked"—"It was not the custom"—"It was a quiet clean stable yard, but no ladies went to such places." My wife positively refused to take a lesson in the proprieties of her sex from a horse jockey in the back settlements of America; and insisted that it was more decorous that she should accompany her husband to a stable, than remain alone in a bar room. In consequence, our guide was near deserting us as companions discreditable to himself. But the hope of profit overcame his sense of propriety; and, at length, he went on with us,—muttering that the shame was ours, and that, after all, people could only say that we were Britishers who did not understand the decencies of life.

The owner of the stable seemed to be doing business on a large scale. He had twenty or thirty horses in his sheds, which were excellently-well kept: but my wife's perverse indelicacy in accompanying her husband to look at the carriage horses he wished to buy, proved to the stablekeeper that we must be quite Johnny Raws and new comers into the civilised world; and he asked what I knew to be three times the value of his beasts.

We walked away, doubting what was next

to be done. Suddenly, my guide accosted a man driving a yellow, cream-coloured horse that was drawing a cart load of stones.

" Will you sell that horse, Mr. James ?"

" I guess I will, if you make it worth my while."

" Where about is the figure ?"

" Well now; I don't want to sell him, because I must have one to do my work, and I shall have to buy another: but there's no denying that this one is a deal too well bred to haul these stones. I reckon you won't have him under a hundred and fifty dollars."

Meanwhile, I was examining the beast in question. It was of a pale yellow cream-colour, not uncommon in that country, with black legs, a magnificent black mane, and a tail that swept the ground. About sixteen hands high; good forequarter; small bone; large joints; short natural tufts of hair on the fetlocks; good barrel; a small head with fiery eyes and flaming red nostrils. It was a beautiful horse; fit for a charger or a light brougham. My jockey whispered to me that he knew the horse; and that it was all right. I had him taken out of the shafts and run along in hand. His paces seemed excellent. He was only five years old.

"If he is all right," I said, "I will give one hundred dollars for him;" and I walked away.

In the course of two hours, I was told that the horse was in the hotel stable, and that the gentleman was waiting for the money.

In much the same manner, on the following day, I picked up a noble dark bay horse with black legs: he was six years old, about one inch higher than the buff, with a somewhat larger and shorter body; with high action, full of fire and speed. For this, I gave ninety dollars.

I had much difficulty in getting a wagon to my taste. I had, of course, understood that I was to have a spring wagon; but was now assured that no springs could stand the roughness of the roads I should have to pass: and in evidence of this, I was taken to see those of the stage coaches. Sure enough, no iron entered into their composition; but the body of the carriage swung from side to side on the thickest possible doubled and quintupled leathern thongs. To a wagon without springs, we had, therefore, to resign ourselves. I was taken to see several; but they all came from Illinois State, and were too narrow in the body to suit my agricultural tastes:—for we had planned that the horses would serve our turn during the following winter at St. Louis, in whatever carriage the fashion of the city might offer, while the wagon could be laid by until required on my son's "location." At length, I found an emigrant German wheelwright who had just finished a wagon that was much after my own European imaginings. I suggested some additions, and paid for the whole as follows:—to some, who may think of emigrating, these details may be useful:—

Indianapolis, June 26, 1851.

To S. HETSELGESER. Dr.

	Dolls.	Cents.
For one wagon	65	0
,, bed	9	0
Making seat	1	0
Step and staples for the seat . .	1	0
Making bows (for the cover) . .	2	0
Four removes of shoes . . .	0	50
	78	50

I bought a drag and chain for two dollars more, and a capital cover of drill, made up complete, for three dollars and thirty-five cents. Nothing was then wanting to our outfit but harness and a whip. Here, I believe, I was rather extravagant. I had first bought a set of ordinary harness which, when brought to the hotel, I had refused to pay for until my horse jockey friend should be able to inspect it and say that it was complete: but the saddler had no idea that an emigrant, who had bought wagon and horses, should not be able to look over and understand his own harness; and, therefore, carried it back to his shop—naturally supposing that I had intended to clap it on the horses and drive away without payment. I had, therefore, to go to another tradesman; and was seduced into purchasing a very tidy set of new, light, wagon harness, for which I gave twenty dollars, and the very dandiest whip that emigrant ever handled. It cost me three dollars and a half; and I was so proud of it, that I carried it back to the hotel myself; and, soon after, had my horses decked in their new gear and harnessed to my new wagon, that I might try the whole in proper style. The black ostler held their heads admiringly, as I mounted the bench, which I had had swung from side to side, in front, as a driving seat. I turned into the High Street of Indianapolis: and what a dash I cut! The horses pawed and pranced; and away we flew, at a capital pace! They were stepping beautifully together and lifting high their fore legs, when a gentleman on horseback rode after me and stopped me.

" I say, stranger!" he cried; " what will you sell them two horses for?"

I tossed my head disdainfully and drove on: but twice more, before I got to the end of the street, was I stopped by the same question from other people. I returned to the inn delighted. I had not thought a wagoner could be so proud of his team!

Some of our boxes had need to be repaired; and I sent for a carpenter to the hotel. A native American came with his man. I was much struck with the manner and cleverness with which he handled his tools. He had made me a new packing case which had to be nailed down, planed and fitted. In Europe four tools would have been required for this—a gimlet, a hammer, a plane, and a pair of pincers: here one sufficed. He never thought of using a gimlet, but struck the nails in, unerringly, with the hammer-shaped end of his adze; a slit in this sufficed to draw out old nails with; while the adze itself answered the purpose of a plane. I never saw carpenter get through his work more neatly and so expeditiously.

"But," said he, "I reckon that you are not British; you have not the accent of the Irish and Scotch, and you do not talk like the English; what country do you come from?"

"We are English," I replied; "all born and raised, as you call it, in England."

"Impossible! you do not talk English like true British."

"What is the difference?"

"You do not say 'ouse' and 'and' for house and hand: all the children, and all of you, pronounce all these words like Americans, and not as real English emigrants pronounce them. Their way of speaking makes us always say that we talk better English than the English themselves."

I had, indeed, often heard the Americans

laughed at for saying so; but now the matter was explained. My carpenter repeated with great accuracy, various instances of provincialisms and vulgarisms which he, and all of them, had noticed, more or less, in all the English emigrants who had come amongst them. Seeing none of any other class, they naturally supposed that all English people pronounced the language in the same manner; and so prided themselves upon the superiority of American English. For, notwithstanding the disagreeable nasal tone and drawling whine in which most of them speak, and notwithstanding a few national phrases and the peculiar use and pronunciation of certain words, it must be admitted that the American people, in general, speak English without provincial dialect or vulgarisms. Whence, in fact, could they acquire such? since all the emigrants they see come from different parts of England, the provincialisms of the one neutralise those of the other.

The wages of a good journeyman carpenter or smith here are from one to one and a half dollar per day, besides board. I paid my

CHAP. X.—INDIANAPOLIS. 281

carpenter a two dollar note, which, after a few hours, he brought back, saying that he could not pass it—that people said it was a forgery. I replied that he should have looked at it when he took it; that I could not tell whether it was the same I gave him or not. Mr. Turtle, however, informed me that the oath of the receiver was always taken as evidence of that question in a court of justice. The note was examined by every one in the bar: some said it was genuine, some not. I afterwards paid it away without question to a branch of the bank by which it purported to have been issued.

During my stay here, other lands had been recommended to me. I will copy the descriptions I received. Such familiarise one with a foreign country, and help to bring its ways before the mind:—

180 acres, of which 65 cleared, in Switzerland county, good house : price, seven thousand dollars.

240 acres, Carrol county, wood : one thousand dollars.

200 acres, near Maddison, unimproved : one hundred and ten dollars per acre.

640 acres in Posey county, two miles from the Ohio.

400 in Knox county, overflowing Wabash bottom, ten miles from Vincennes.

500 in Clay and Owen, in the valley of Eel River, one or two miles of canal from Terre Haute to Evansville.

Then I had letters from Illinois, one of which recommended to me " a tract of land of 1300 acres, with about 70 or 80 acres of improved land upon it, with a commodious dwelling 46 feet by 50 feet, two and a half stories, frame, good cellars, the two first stories four fine rooms in each; a hall in each story. The third story," I continue to quote the letter, " is deck roof, with at least a dozen small rooms. Orchard adjoining, and tolerable barn. A quarter of a mile distant, in another part of the farm, is one of the best barns in this county, with cellar: the barn is 74 feet by 54 feet, and a comfortable dwelling hard by. This property, I think, can be purchased for four thousand dollars or thereabouts; the improvements are worth more than the above amount, and have cost at least double as much.

CHAP. X.—INDIANAPOLIS. 283

Should you wish for more than the above land in this tract, there is plenty for sale adjoining which you can purchase at from one dollar to six dollars per acre. There is no part of the western country more healthy.

"The land mentioned is eight miles from Schauneetown, on the railroad in the direction of St. Louis. The railroad was projected some fourteen years ago, and abandoned, and is now used as a state road. The main dwelling is forty rods from the road: the smaller dwelling and main barn are on the road."

Such letters as the above (which, to one who has been in the backwoods, bring the whole scene before the mind in the vividness of true description) such letters as the above, proved to me that it would be unwise to determine hastily upon anything. I had much to see in Illinois; and I determined to make Vandalia, the capital of that state, my headquarters for a week or two.

Some readers may like to know how a newspaper is conducted in the backwoods. For these, I will describe a number of the *Daily Indiana State Sentinel*, which I brought away with me. It is printed on very fair paper, about as large as the English *Globe*, and is " published every evening at five dollars per annum in advance"—not quite one guinea a year. The rates of advertisements are said to be " fifty cents for eight lines or less, one insertion, and twenty-five cents for each additional insertion: announcing candidates for office, one dollar each line: all advertisements for charitable institutions, fire companies, ward, township, and other public meetings and such like to be charged half price: marriages and deaths inserted without charge: obituary notices and funeral invitations to be charged half price."

After a report of the California Democratic Convention, the first page is filled with advertisements which are intended to be as attractive as possible. I say nothing of the three Insurance Companies which compete for public favour: nor of the railroads that preface their notices by little prints of smoking engines, which show, by the by, the driver, as everywhere on American lines, standing under a shade to protect him from the sun and the rain: I say nothing of the Odd Fellows and

Freemasons, who issue their notices amid eyes and hands and hearts, and suns and triangles and compasses, which they alone understand: I say nothing of the convenient tables, which tell the hours at which all mails arrive at and leave Indianapolis, the statement when the different courts will hold their respective sessions, or of the bank report of the current value of notes and moneys; or of the yearly almanack: but my eye is caught by the pretty little prints of gentlemen making their best bows and little boys walking hand-in-hand—all sprucely drest and calling attention to so many clothing emporiums; of stoves announcing "Something new which cannot be beat — Jenny Lind's cooking stove"; and of a great boot upon wheels, smoking like the funnel of a steam engine, and followed by four shoes of different sizes racing after it on wheels, while "Fairbanks" exclaims, " Clear the track !" and bids you "call and examine for yourself" his supply of boots and shoes.

But, leaving the pictorial advertisements, I own that I like the matter of fact, business style of the others, which go strait to the point without circumlocution. Messrs. Robins or Daniel Smith and Son would, doubtless, be scandalized by the advertisement of an estate agent, which begins with the following modest phraseology: "I am authorized by the Probate Court to make sale of the following real estate:" and, after describing the property in quiet language and quiet type, concludes thus:—" I can be found at my residence four miles south-east of Jacksonville, and letters addressed to Wallace, Fountain County, will reach me, J. A. White." Our great auctioneers would think it impossible to introduce properties, and, still less, themselves to the world without the bombast of large type and advertisements costing five pounds each, or something thereabouts:—(I have had to dispute the bill of one of them, which charged upwards of eight hundred pounds for advertizing and offering for sale an estate on which he only sold the household furniture:)—and yet the Americans manage to do business notwithstanding.

What can be more curt and intelligible than the following:—

"Ladies! I have this day received a new

assortment of fine ribbons, silks, lawns, bareges, de laines, etc. Please call and examine them at the cheap store of H. Parrish."

" CHEESE. A good supply constantly on hand at V. Hanna and Co.'s."

" Wanted. 50,000 pounds of bacon, for which the market price in cash will be paid by Blythe and Holland."

I own, however, that I do not understand the following:—" Vices—superior quality at reduced prices. Call at Wainwright and Brothers." In Europe, vices are not advertised for sale. We have not any.

Let it not, however, be supposed that all American advertisements are as condensed as those I have quoted: I give them as samples of a particular style; some are almost as florid as Moses and Son themselves could desire; but the earnestness of men of business is the characteristic of most of them. Amongst other advertisements, I see that the governor of Indiana makes proclamation of one hundred dollars reward " for the capture of a man charged with murder, who had broken jail; (in England it would have been pounds instead of dollars, with no greater likelihood of catching him); and the list of tolls payable on the " Central Plankroad", but which, however, were not to be exacted from those " going to or returning from Militia musterings, from any religious meeting on the Sabbath, or from any state, town, or county election, or from any funeral procession."

It is not such a barbarous country, after all! This reference to funeral processions reminds me of the style of American newspaper obituary. Much trouble and inquiry, at a time of family distress, is avoided by the usual addition to the notice of death, which says where and at what hour the funeral will take place, and that " the relatives and friends are respectfully invited to attend without further invitation:" then, if the deceased is connected with any other part of the country, Wisconsin State, for example, a notice usually follows, thus, " Wisconsin papers please copy."

But my *Indiana State Sentinel* is not entirely given up to advertisements: here are leading articles and paragraphs on matters of general political interests in much the same style and of the average ability of those we should meet with in English provincial papers. If any difference is visible in them, it is that they are more courteous to their contemporaries, and deal less in the vein of the *Eatanswill Gazette* than our own country press. I have read a paragraph in a New York paper which announced the publication of another opposition paper which would take quite a different line in politics, and said, that the editor of the new organ was a man of so great ability, that it, the old established paper, could not doubt of the success it wished him. This was not the greeting which our established papers give to new adventurers.

In the *Indiana Sentinel*, there is the following notice, which is characteristic of the country and shews the scarcity of servants: " Our carrier has been sick for the past few days, and we have been unable to procure a competent one to fill his place. We hope our subscribers will be patient if any errors should occur in delivering the papers, and if they will call at the office we will rectify them. Our carrier will probably be able to resume his duties on to-morrow."

Those who study educational statistics may be interested in drawing comparisons with the statement that, according to the report of the visiting committee, the numbers of children attending the various Sunday schools in Indianapolis during the past month were 1818
Promised to send - - - - 70
Refused to send - - - - - 32

Total number of children in the city - 1920

When, in England, shall we see all the children, except one hundred and two, attend the Sunday schools attached to the different churches in a city of upwards of eight thousand inhabitants? In my parish, in Devonshire, the only school is the one attached to the parish church : and the clergyman refused permission to attend it to children who had been baptized by dissenting teachers.

Thus, although in the backwoods, it must not be supposed that we had no evidence of refinement in Indianapolis. The men, it is true, dressed sensibly in grey holland coats and vests; I bought a suit myself, which is still my comfort in hot weather: but the ladies were as refined and elegant as in New York. The druggists, and storekeepers, had every sort of Parisian perfumery and female elegancies on sale: French gloves, eau de Cologne, and everything that an European *élégante* could require. We rejoiced in this evidence of their prosperity and leisure, as we replenished the bottles and drawers of our family medicine chest. Then, little anticipating how soon we should be obliged to have recourse to them, light of heart and full of hope, we clambered up into our new wagon, and [on this very day three years—I am writing on the 27th of June, 1854] our beautiful horses started forth, with a will, on our journey across the prairies of Illinois to the banks of the mighty Mississippi.

CHAPTER XI.

THE WAGON.

Our new equipage.—Its triumphs and pleasures.—Highway robbers.—Baiting.—The Cholera House.—Long's House.—An American woman.—Mount Meridian.—The National Road.—Mr. Townsend.—Evening fancies.—Records of children.—Dr. Ushaw's.—A land-jobber.—Van Buren.—Premonitory symptoms.

I HAD hired Morrison, as the man who had helped me to purchase my horses and wagon was called, to convey our luggage with his own two horses and wagon from Indianapolis to Vandalia. A heavy load it was for his miserable cattle; and as he started with it from the door of Wright's House, I doubted whether they would be able to accomplish what he had undertaken: but he was to hire additional horses if necessary. Carpet-bags and such light articles, were thrown into the bottom of our own wagon; as we thought that they would make convenient seats for the children. The body of the vehicle was then filled half way up

CHAP. XI.—THE WAGON.

with hay and straw, that they might less feel the shaking and the jolting. The cages of the parrot and of the canary birds were tied to the hoops, on which the canvas awning was stretched, overhead: and, amid much fun and laughter, the children helped, lifted and tumbled one another into their places. My wife and I scrambled up to the bench, which I had had made and swung across, on straps, under the awning in front. I handled my beautiful whip and shook the reins; and away our horses started at a good trot. The Indianapolitans looked after us admiring, and thought we had a most perfect turn out for the prairie and the backwoods.

"How little," said my wife to me, as she pressed my arm, " how little happiness is dependent upon the external attributes of wealth or rank! According to my earliest recollections of travel, I always rode on an elephant, and was surrounded with body guards—when my father was deputed to the Nepaul country after the war. Since then, have I ever watched the building of a carriage in Long Acre, or driven in May Fair, with as much pleasure as that with which we have marked the finishing of this wagon in the wheelwright's shop, and are now starting on our travels through the Far West?"

We were, in truth, very happy.

But how felt our children?

"How delightful we all thought it for the first five minutes!" writes Louie. "Eleven children packed in straw, with carpet-bags and dressing-cases filling up the crevices, and a canvas awning over our heads! In the exuberance of our spirits, we all sang, 'In the days when we went gypseying.' But, in a very short time, complaints and murmurs began to arise from all parties. 'How the wagon jolts!' cried one: 'How burning hot the sun is through the top!' exclaimed another: 'How uncomfortable it is not to have any seats!' said a third, moving impatiently."……

"Before we had been three yards," writes Lucy, "Polly's cage began swinging backwards and forwards amongst us, knocking the heads on each side of it; and the poor little canaries were jolted off their perches to the bottom of their own cage. That we might not incommode the person opposite to each of us, we were obliged to draw our feet under us, like tailors, or to sit upon our heels; but then, if we leant against the sides of the wagon, we felt that the skin would soon be rubbed off our shoulders by its jolting. Fancy our position; with two little children tumbling in the hay and crawling over everybody, and that dreadful cage thumping our heads!"

"We had all looked forwards with impatience," writes Agnes, " to the day of starting afresh on our journey, and to the pleasures of the wagon. At last, our equipage came to the door; and, with a little squeezing, the whole number found room to sit, some on the hay on the floor and some on carpet bags. In the town, our spirits rose even higher, and we enjoyed the jolting on the pavement; but as we found it did not abate, we soon began to tire of it; and those who, for the sake of novelty, had wished to sit on hay, were glad to change their places with those who were on bags. But as not even that position brought the pleasure they had expected, an unpleasant conviction very soon forced itself into our minds—namely, that travelling in a wagon on American roads was not the most agreeable way of progressing; which, of course, we had thought it would be. But what, was our surprise, a little way out of Indianapolis, just as we were beginning to resign ourselves to the jolting, to find it cease suddenly! On looking out from under the awning, to discover the cause of this unexpected change, we found that we were travelling on a plank road. This, to our great joy, continued some miles; during which our anticipations of the pleasures of travelling in a wagon were partly realized: although we could not help wishing sometimes, as the heat of the day advanced, that the wagon had been made a little wider."

Partly to give our children more room, and partly as a guard to our baggage, I sent Kenelm, who was nearly sixteen and the eldest of my boys then with us, to ride in the wagon with the heavy goods and Morrison, who, I found, could not travel as fast as I did. Morrison, indeed, had suggested that we ought to carry a couple of revolvers with us, to use in case of an attack from robbers. I had laughed at the proposal, and asked him if he thought Americans would turn highway robbers in order to pillage clothes, linen and books, and such other heavy luggage : but the man shook his head mysteriously, and intimated that he believed our boxes to contain goods of a different description. I had then asked Colonel Drake his opinion of the need of firearms; but was assured by him that a highway robbery was scarcely ever heard of in the state. He himself, he said, rode and drove through the country alone at all hours of the day and night, when he was known to have large sums of government money about him; but he had never felt cause for the least anxiety. I had started, therefore, without the revolvers; and if I now sent Kenelm to the other wagon, it was more that he might hold a horse or carry a message in case of need, than from any fear of banditti.

A pragmatical idiot was that Morrison. He was an Irishman by birth; but though he had been a matter of thirty years in America, he professed to have known and to remember all about English people and their ways; and pretended to discover that we were not of the common class of emigrants, and to treat us with immense respect. Then he had been a schoolmaster in his youth; and he would force, upon my boy, endless discussions not only on the English but on the Latin grammar likewise, of which he remembered a few words. He thought himself very learned; and no less a man of the world and knowing in the ways of America, than he was learned: and I soon found that he considered himself personally offended whenever I did anything in the slightest degree contrary to his advice.

But we soon left him and his wagon behind, as we trotted lightly along this plank road. And very pleasant a plank road is to travel upon. It may be slippery in wet weather: but now it saved us from the dust which would have arisen from gravel; and the sawn boards or planks, about three inches thick, being nailed to sleepers at the two sides of the road, spanned it from side to side, and rose and sank under us with the elasticity of the floor of a ball room. On each side of the plank track, between it and the worm fences that bounded the road, were holes and stumps and ditches and natural water courses that no wheels could venture amongst.

The road continued in a nearly straight direction through a pleasant country, in which cultivated spots amid the woods and prairies grew more and more rare. There was a good deal of traffic on the road; quite as much as would be seen on a turnpike road in England; but it was confined entirely to rough-and-ready carriages or agricultural teams: all these went at a trot—more or less fast. Plough horses, in all this country, get over nearly five miles an hour:—with less of fatigue to themselves than our heavy English teams creep over two miles. We passed, also, several wagons loaded with emigrants: some with their bedding and articles of furniture. Our horses attracted considerable notice, as being better than those usually driven by emigrants; but in other respects, our equipage was entirely like those used in the country, and passed without the slightest regard. This was what we wished.

About one o'clock, I pulled up at a little

inn in a little village named Springfield, where I had been advised to bait. My horses were unharnessed and taken into a shed, the floor and litter of which the man who attended them first thoroughly sprinkled and saturated with water. He told me this was necessary to keep down the fleas that would otherwise devour the horses. Returning to the inn, I mentioned this to my wife, who reminded me that the same plan had always been followed in the rooms she had occupied in Turkey, on her journey from Constantinople to Vienna across the Balkan, when she had slept, for twenty-three nights, on straw laid over mud floors. Such are the pleasures of travelling for pleasure!

I had cautioned my family not to complain of the jolting of the wagon, lest it should appear that they had never ridden in one before; and in answer to the usual string of interrogatories, to assume the character of emigrants going from Cincinnati to Illinois. I now found them in a little sitting room, furnished with a few books and a rocking sofa, seated round a dirty tablecloth, and swallowing, with such appetite as wagons give, a dinner consisting of broiled ham, bread, good honey in the honey-comb, and coffee. The landlady was standing by, fanning them all with a peacock's tail; and I heard the following dialogue between her and my wife:—

"I suppose now you come from Cincinnati and are going West?"

This was assented to.

"What's your name?"

It was told.

"I don't remember such a name. There was a Mrs. West who kept a school at Cincinnati, but she's been dead these three year."

"I am not a school mistress."

"No! well now, I thought you was. What are all these young folk?"

"My children."

"Well now, I shouldn't think so if you didn't say so. You don't look old enough to have all these children. You've a good lot of them, to be sure! You've been married some time, I s'pose?"

This was sufficiently evident. Although Dr. Johnson did say that the Americans multiplied with the rapidity of their own rattlesnakes, her asking such a question proved that our landlady's interrogative powers were well nigh exhausted: and as we had also fallen in her estimation since my wife had denied being a schoolmistress, she soon left us comparatively to ourselves.

After a rest of three hours, we started again; and traversing a country road much like that of the forenoon, arrived at a village, where I was much pleased to find a large respectable-looking hotel. Here we had planned to pass the night; and it was with some dismay that I discovered that all the blinds and shutters of the house were closed. No one answered my summons: but people came to their several doors in the village and gazed upon us. I went to some of them, and ascertained that the mistress of the house had died, the day before, of cholera, and that her husband had shut up the premises and had left; but they offered to find the managing waiter, who, perhaps, could let us in and fix us up for the night. Imagine our feelings on hearing this offer to be let into the house where, I believe, the cholera-stricken corpse still lay unburied! The stage coach from Indianapolis drove into the town and stopped to change horses; and I hastened to take counsel of the driver. Sure enough, the landlord had deserted the premises; for he had travelled by that coach the night before, and the driver believed several others besides the mistress had died in the house; but he assured me that I should find very good quarters at a place called Long's House, about three miles further on.

We started again; but tired and terrified at what we had heard. The sun was setting, and we thought those three miles interminable. The country became more wild; the road more broken; yet onwards we toiled. Dark fir woods covered the little we could see of the country; and day was closing in as the longed-for Long's House loomed in sight. It was a single house. My children hurried out of the wagon, and into a neat parlour on the ground floor, where was a bed in a recess.

"On the table," writes Louie, "lay several books of fashions, magazines, and other books, which I looked over. I had just begun to interest myself in a German ghost story, when a young woman with long ringlets came in and, taking the book from me, said 'I wish you'd let those books alone, and not go spoiling them that way.' So saying, she left the room, slamming the door after her. At that moment, our youngest brother, who had been asleep on one of our sisters' lap, woke up and began crying for some tea, he was so thirsty. Mama was trying to pacify him, when papa came into the room with the landlady."

I had, in fact, driven my wagon to the side of the road, and followed Mr. Long as he led my horses into a large barn at the bottom of his farmyard. Here I had had to consult with him how many ears of Indian corn the horses ought to have with their oats; for it seemed to be considered necessary that they should have some, and to be dangerous to give them too many. The ears were to be paid for at so much each. Mr. Long was an Irishman, who had emigrated many years before; he had married an American, by whom he had a grown-up daughter: he was very civil, but, apparently, melancholy and timid. This I could account for when I became acquainted with his wife and daughter. For, when I now accompanied her into the little room where all my family were congregated, and we asked her to show us our bedrooms, she drily answered that she could not spare us any.

"Where, then, are we to sleep?" I asked.

"Oh, you can sleep here, can't you?" she replied.

"What! father, mother, and eleven children?"

"Well, now, if you can't sleep here, I calculate that you must sleep in the wagon."

I had already discovered that, to get even money's worth in these countries, it was necessary to adopt a system of canvassing; to treat every one as one would an unwilling or hostile voter in an English election. Fortunately, we had had experience in such matters; and drawing the cross-grained old woman aside, my wife and I began to butter and coax her with soft sawder, as if we hoped to get her to plump for us. The infernal hag at last so far relented as to place one other, a large double-bedded room, at our disposal. We hurried some of our children into it, to secure it, while others went out to the wagon to fetch in their carpet-bags and dressing-cases;—afraid to ask the woman of the house to assist them, lest she should take the room from them again. We now begged to have tea.

"But what do you want tea for?"

"Because," I said, "we have had nothing to eat since two o'clock, and the children are very hungry."

"Well, now; you should have come earlier; for we have all finished this long time; and you would not have us fix it up again, would you?"

Again we had recourse to the "butter" and "soft sawder"; and again, but with greater difficulty, we persuaded mother and daughter to give us what we needed. They boiled the kettle and spread a cloth in another room; whining through their noses and talking at us during the whole time. Once, I unluckily said a few words in praise of their meek husband and father, who wisely stayed with the horses in the stable; my praise only turned their talk against all emigrants and Irishmen.

CHAP. XI.—THE WAGON.

Meanwhile, Morrison arrived with the luggage wagon and silently drew it up beside the road. He then unharnessed his horses and tied them to a paling; and the first words he spoke to any one, were addressed to the landlord who had come out to greet him:—

"Well, colonel; good evening. Can you oblige me with a few oats and a score of corn heads for these horses?"

"Will you not put them in the stable?" I asked.

"What would be the good? It is a fine warm night. Why should I pay for stable room?"

Our six girls, with their two baby brothers, now took possession of the room which our tactics had won from the she-dragons, Mother and Daughter Long. Our three elder boys went out to pass the night amid the hay in the bottom of our wagon; and I and my wife were left to our parlour down stairs.

"There were two large beds in our room," writes Lucy; "and we took off one of the mattresses and laid it on the floor for our elder sisters, Catharine and Ellen, and for little

Isabel. Agnes and Louie took one of the beds, and I had the other for myself and my two baby brothers. I was waked up, about twenty times during the night, by first one baby kicking me on one side and then the other on the other side. Sometimes they would throw themselves across me; sometimes one of them would kick me in the face in his restless sleep. I had not much rest or sleep that night; but poor Ellen was worse off than I. Each time I woke, she was either tossing about the bed or walking up and down the room, with the toothache, afraid of disturbing Catherine. It was with joy we heard a clock strike six, and we all got up immediately, tired as we were. But here a new difficulty arose :—there was neither bason, jug, water, nor towels in the room. We asked our kind hostess to give us some, and she asked, in her usual querulous tone :—

" But what do you want them for ?"

" To wash ourselves with."

" Well, then; you can't have them, for we hav'n't any."

" But what are we to do ?"

CHAP. XI.—THE WAGON.

" You can go down to the yard and you'll find a pump and a towel."

" We did not relish the idea," continues Lucy; " so Ellen dressed herself and went down, and found the daughter of the old woman, and represented to her how she had been suffering all night after a fatiguing day; and how unpleasant it would be to begin another day without making any ablutions. After talking to her thus for a long time—but with the greatest politeness—she succeeded in obtaining from her a small tin pie-dish and a towel : she then went to the pump, and filled the dish with water, and brought her prizes up to us. Imagine what a splendid washing we had in the pie-dish !"

This morning Mrs. Long and her daughter positively refused to give us any breakfast. " It was too much trouble." " There were too many of us." " She had something else to do." " She did not care for our money." And " there was a good hotel one mile further on." The last motive encouraged us to let her have her own way; and we left her. I forget all the woes that I imprecated on her head : but my feelings are now calmed down, and as, no doubt, the two women have worried their husband and father to death, I now only wish that the daughter may have married some sturdy German emigrant who beats both her and her mother once a week, and compels them to wash themselves. The libellers! why, according to their showing, American women (they themselves were American born) American women, in the station of farmers' wives, know no other ablutions than what they administer to themselves at the pump in the yard! Can this be true?

In a quarter of an hour, we came to the house where Mrs. Long had assured us we should get a good breakfast. It was a log cottage of the poorest kind, beside a dark forest of small Scotch firs. For curiosity, I asked what provisions they had: plenty of whiskey and a little corn bread. But Mount Meridian was only half a dozen miles further; and, in this pretty little village, we found a decent public house, the poor woman of which set out for us a tolerable breakfast, and attended on us as well as she could. But she too was suffering from the toothache; and was soon obliged to betake herself to the chimney corner, where she sat smoking a pipe of tobacco in the hope of relieving the pain.

After Mount Meridian, we found our road change sadly for the worse. It is true that it is marked in all the maps as the "National Road" leading from east to west in an almost straight line—from Pittsburgh to St. Louis: and it had been fenced in and laid down as such: but Congress, by subsequent decision, declared that the making and maintaining of roads was not a national affair, but should be at the charge of each State that wanted them. The condition of this repudiated road, now, therefore, depended upon the wants and the traffic of each township through which it passed. The tract of country after passing Mount Meridian was but thinly inhabited: the road was little used, and still less attention was given to keep it up. The water tables on each side were choked or washed away: water courses ran down the middle of it or furrowed it deep from side to side, or dug it into wide pits. Sometimes, these had to be passed through almost on stepping stones: sometimes, the rain-channels were bridged over by planks, so short that there was not an inch to spare at the side of each wheel. Sometimes, where the gravelly top soil was quite worn away, and a quicksandy bottom exposed beneath, a track, just wide enough for the wheels, was made by a corduroy road laid across the bog. I have already explained the construction of a plank road: the difference between it and a corduroy road is much the same as that between a log and a frame house. A corduroy road is made of the unhewn boles of trees laid side by side on the earth. A slip is nailed across each end to keep them in their places: and the wheels, whether of carriage or wagon, fall from bole to bole with the regularity of the thumps and stops with which the cogs in the wheels of a watch play into and arrest one another. Sometimes, the hollow between each prostrate trunk of a tree is partially filled up by earth; and then, of course, the jolts are less severe.

My horses were rather too spirited for this work; and it was with great difficulty I could restrain and guide them. I was very proud of the Jehuship with which I threaded the intricacies of the " National Road": I have since driven across the St. Gothard Alps; but this was the more difficult feat of the two.

We went down to a brook, where they were building the foundations of a bridge, and up its prettily wooded banks on the other side, where a nice looking house, called, I think, the Stag House, hung out its signboard. Soon after this, our road led us into the beautiful parklike grounds of a forest; and here all traces of it suddenly ceased. Not a track was to be seen on the smooth green turf beneath the tall, shady oak trees. The fresh breezes, that came to us as from its deep shades, were delightful. We would willingly have lingered here a-gypsying; but our journey lay before us. Some citizens, driving wagons, pointed out the track to me. It led down to the side of a pretty stream, I believe some of the head waters of the White River. They were rather deep; but we forded them, and clambered up on the other side. Here many scores of labourers were at work on cuttings and embankments for the railroad from Indianapolis to St. Louis.

The weather was intolerably hot, and our children and horses suffered much, notwithstanding the fine prairie breeze that met us. I, indeed, complained that it chilled and gave me the rheumatism, as it blew through the tunnel shaped awning of our wagon, and whistled round my shoulders and loins, clad, as they were, in the new thin Indianapolis suit of brown holland: but I had felt griping pains and uneasiness all the morning, which may have accounted for this. What, however, was our surprise and delight to find, at the distance of every four miles along this miserable road, amid the backwoods of America, public wells and pumps, supplied with buckets for the use of cattle, and tin cups from which to assuage human thirst! Here was the ancient civilization and kind feeling of the East transplanted into the almost untrodden wilderness of the Far West! I have doubted whether we drank too unsparingly at these wells; but I do not think so. I myself was already ill.

Our children suffered severely from the

CHAP. XI.—THE WAGON.

roughness of the road, as the consequent jolting of the wagon was rendered almost intolerable. " Polly's cage," writes Lucy, " had threatened our heads with dreadful knocks, so that I had been obliged to hold it with both hands to steady it; but now, instead of the cage hitting me, I was thrown against the cage; and I really do not know which I preferred, but I think the former. I almost fancy that I can still feel the bruises I then received. Now was the time when all our different characters and dispositions were shown. The most patient and good-tempered were, Catherine, the eldest; Frank, the second brother with us; and Isabel, who was the youngest of us girls, but yet so much older than the two baby boys that we seemed as two families. When one or other had a headache, Catherine would take him or her and lay them in a comfortable place by her own side, and then read aloud a chapter out of à Kempis' *Imitation of Christ*, by way of checking the discontent of another or of all. When we went slow enough, Frank would get out and walk, in order to make more room for the others, and, heedless of the heat himself, would pick and bring flowers to break the monotony of our drive. And Isabel, who was nine years old, would take the two babies to herself, and try to keep them amused by telling stories quietly to them in one corner of the wagon."

We stopped to bait and dine this day at a village containing about two score of houses, to one of the best of which we were invited by a signboard inscribed " Townsend House"; and a very comfortable little farmhouse it was, neat and clean, and but recently built, of red brick. The son of the landlord was married, and lived in the well whitewashed log-house close beside it. There his father had first settled in the backwoods. With an air of great condescension, the son assisted me to take the harness from my horses, and to give them their corn in the stable. But the father, mother, and daughters, were exceedingly civil and attentive : they laid us out a comparatively-excellent dinner on a very white tablecloth, and stood and chatted with us, and fanned us with peacocks' tails the while we ate. All this was done with a manner perfectly respectful to us but as perfectly self-respectful to themselves, —a genuine American manner of the best sort. They gave us what we wanted, and we were to remunerate them for it. Having announced that they kept open house, it was so far their duty to make their guests welcome; but here was no cringing for custom, no expression of excessive gratitude: the obligation on both sides was mutual.

But Mr. Townsend was an independent man: he had evidently an estate the produce of which had brought up his family, settled his eldest son, and built himself a good new house and outbuildings. True, he had a publican's sign before his door; but this was put up with the intention of keeping off guests rather than of attracting them. Paradoxical as it may seem, such is the motive and object of the signs before these lone farmhouses in the West. The tide of emigrants sets past them. Hospitality would forbid them to turn from their doors people who might ask for food and shelter. They would be obliged, therefore, to receive all applicants to their board and hearth. By putting up a sign and announcing themselves as publicans, they will, at least, keep away those who cannot pay for respectable accommodation.

Mr. Townsend and I spoke of the railway then in progress near him. He was surprised, he said, to discover the wealth of the farmers. "We have been waiting, sir," he exclaimed, "for the monied men of the towns to do the work; but we have now found out our strength; they may drop it or go on with it as they like; we shall complete it ourselves and for our own benefit."

How strange it was to hear a farmer in the backwoods of America thus assert the benefit of railroads to his class, while I remembered the difficulties experienced in making them through purely agricultural districts in England, and even the opposition so often shown to them by our wealthy landowners! The railroad in this neighbourhood was being made almost entirely by Irish labourers. Of them, my landlord spoke as I had often before heard Americans speak of the Irish:—

"They make our railroads and docks and drink our whisky. An Englishman, a Scotchman, a German—all settle down into good citizens: an Irish emigrant scarcely ever does so. The Germans make very quiet, good citizens."

Can a people that has been oppressed and degraded in every possible way, and purposely, for centuries, be expected to use its freedom, when it suddenly escapes from its fetters, as those who have never worn them? The Scotch and the Germans have, for example, been educated for generations: for generations, even hedge teachers for the Irish have been proscribed.

I believe it was the unpleasant feeling within me that gave me a yearning for something to drink here stronger than water, and I crossed the street of the village to a store where I saw a printed bill recommending a beverage it called "Cronk". I had seen this advertized in every village we had passed, and highly puffed. Wishing also to become acquainted with a tipple unknown in Europe, I had a bottle opened for me. It fizzed up like gingerbeer: but the taste was so unpalatable that I set down the glass undrunk. The mortified vender (perhaps it was the Dr. Cronk himself, who, they told me, had invented it) refused to take the few cents, the price of the bottle.

Newspapers, periodical publications, and Methodist hymn-books, were, as usual, lying about the parlour of this neat farmhouse; and as my Louie was not here inhibited from looking at them, she would as willingly as myself have lingered longer with its intelligent inmates. "In the forenoon," she writes, "we had found every hour that we spent in the wagon more intolerable than the last, and we had heartily wished ourselves at our journey's end. I had suffered from such a pain in my side that I had been obliged to lie down amongst the carpet bags, and try to sleep, for it was increased much by the jolting of the wagon; but when we again proceeded, in the cool evening air, our spirits rose, and we began twining round our bonnets some of the wild flowers and feathers that our brothers had brought us, as we all joined in singing the French cantiques that we had learned at Talence. How delighted would have been the heart of any good French emigrant priest had he

CHAP. XI.—THE WAGON.

chanced to pass by, and heard the beautiful cantique,

'Crois, en Dieu créateur du ciel et de la terre,
Qui conserve et gouverne en maître l'univers,'

thus sung by the inmates of a wagon in the backwoods of America! I bethought me how, forgetting his exile, he would have fancied himself once more in his own beloved France, surrounded by the village girls singing their favourite hymn;—how he would have heard once more, in imagination, the bells of his own little village church,—until, recalled by the setting of the sun in front of him, he would have started to say the prayer which is said at that moment by three hundred millions of his fellow Catholics in all parts of the globe; and, pausing with us to repeat the holy words, would have remembered where he was, and then with us would have joyfully hurried on towards his resting-place for the night. And so did we also hurry on; and great was our delight to find that we were not to fare as we had on the preceding night: for our present station was a large, clean, comfortable-looking frame-house, with a large garden around it filled with flowers and fruit trees, and with two or three beehives in front.

"A very pretty young woman," Louie continues, "sat at the door nursing her baby. Our mother and eldest sister soon entered into conversation with her. She was very young, and it was her first child; so she, of course, was very proud of it; and it certainly was a very pretty child. In the house, we saw marks of more civilisation than we had noted for some time. There were clean white curtains to the beds, which were covered with very smart patch-work quilts; and all the dressing tables had toilet covers. At tea, we had fruit served in, what was to us quite a new manner:—large quantities of currants were floated in molasses; and this certainly was a great improvement to this otherwise rather sour or tasteless fruit."

I make no apology for giving these frequent extracts from the records of my children. These pages profess to recount the impressions and adventures of a family in a new country. Those impressions can be best conveyed in the language of the several members of the party. Let me not be told that the observations of my children are trivial: trivial observations, such as might escape the notice of the censorious reader or of myself, best show the everyday habits and life of those upon whom they are made. Great historians may describe the great deeds of sovereigns and heroes:—may write history as it has been delivered down to us: but, for want of the records of a different class of observers, how little do we know of the manners and feelings of the people of those very times of which we fancy that we have learned the history! I have undertaken to write the history of a family during a few, to it, eventful months: I appeal to the sympathy of the reader under no false pretences: I myself know that, by following the little adventures of that family, he will acquire a more intimate knowledge of the people amongst whom they occur, than he could gather from whole volumes of professedly-descriptive research; but if his pride revolts from such a means of acquiring information; if he cannot be taught "out of the mouths of babes and sucklings"; if he cannot "suffer little children to come unto" him, and feel an interest in their brotherly love and in the sorrows of their mother—in the unwonted toils and trials heroically borne by all,—let him, at once, close this volume. It is written by no congenial spirits; and I warn him that it will not contain anything suited to his superior intellect.

The house in which my family were now enjoying a luxurious contrast with Mrs. Long's *ménage*, had a sign in front of it which marked it as "Dr. Ushaw's". It had been recommended to me at the place where we had baited. I had been told, what I afterwards discovered to be the fact, that Dr. Ushaw himself was a medical practitioner of no small repute in the district; and that he, also, kept open house in order to avoid intrusive guests. Close to his house, were very good farm buildings and a large yard, into which I drove my team. I was looking about for some one to unharness them, when I saw a stout, good-looking man, without a coat but showing very clean shirt sleeves, and with a broad-brimmed straw hat on his head, drive two or three cows towards the yard from a cleared field beyond. I opened the gate to let them in, and was very civilly greeted by their driver. This I found to be Dr. Ushaw himself. He immediately applied himself to my horses; did all that was needful for them, and then put his shoulder, with a right good will, to the wheels of my wagon and forced it under a wide shed. He complained that he had lately lost his farming man—an Irish emigrant, who had thrown up a settled place, in which he had the high wages that he had himself named, for the adventure and mob-work with his countrymen on the railroad. This, he said, was the way with them all. It was impossible to retain one of them after their first wants were satisfied and their spirits rose. Nor in the indoors, could his wife and daughters persuade any help to stay with them after she was once able to buy ribbons and finery, and had been trained to be sufficiently handy to undertake a situation in a town.

Dr. Ushaw lamented much the ill-feeling that existed in the State against negroes; but so anxious was Indiana to avoid the dangers which many dreaded from the influx of free negroes, that the citizens were even then debating a law to exclude them altogether from their boundaries. Hence free negro servants were more scarce here than in most States of the Union.

I found one inmate in the house, who had been lodging there for some days. He was sipping brandy and water medicinally, as a preservative against cholera, with symptoms of which he had been threatened, and which had detained him here. I joined him in taking the prescribed remedy, and for the same reason : and we sat under the verandah together. He was on his way back to Ohio from a place in the heart of Illinois State ; he did not seem exactly to know where ; but it was from a lot of three or four hundred acres of wood and prairie that he had bought; and he wound up by saying that he only hoped that he should never see it again.

"What could have induced him to purchase it ?" I asked.

He had some spare money that he wished to invest: he had heard of this land, which was to be had at about three dollars an acre: and so he had bought it. The tide of emigration set strong that way; and he had no doubt that, in a very short time, he would be able to sell it again at double the cost price. It was very difficult to get good land cheap in any part of the United States. There were companies in New York, and in all the great towns, which employed agents to buy up for them all the land that was worth having, almost as soon as it was surveyed; and who kept it until they could parcel it out and sell it again at an immense profit.

All this was perfectly true, and showed that Brother Jonathan knows how to make money out of even what is thought to be his most worthless commodity, land.

A poor labourer had been taken ill with cholera just before we arrived; and had been carried to a house within sight of our hotel. My own feelings did not make this comforting intelligence. A dose was mixed for me out of our family medicine chest, and we all retired to bed. After a disturbed night, during which the rest of the family were devoured by musquitos, we all met around a plentifully and neatly-spread breakfast table. My friend, the land speculator, had already departed on his homeward journey. The poor man who had been taken ill of the cholera, was already dead. I paid four dollars and a half for our night's entertainment; and a quarter of a dollar to an ostler, who had, at last, been found for the nonce. Then, pleased with our landlord and his family, but rather damped in our own spirits, we mounted our wagon and pursued our journey.

It was a small straggling village where we had passed the night. A few log cottages, dirty and blackened by time, stood by the side of the high road on the borders of the stunted fir forest. It was called Van Buren. How little we thought that, within three years, the highly-informed, gentlemanly and venerable ex--President from whom it took its name, would be a guest in our drawing-rooms at Rome—talking with us over these scenes of our adventures!

The " national road " was no longer broken up as it had been. Fortunately others, besides the nation, found their advantage in keeping it in order. It ran in a straight line along the table land; then, turning to the right, descended a rather steep hill into the Valley of the Wabash. I had been told that there were two good hotels at Terre Haute—the Prairie House and another. The Prairie was the first house we came to on the outskirts of the town. Surprised to find so large an hotel in such an out-of-the-way part of the world, we determined that it would be unwise to pass it in search of any other possibly better, probably worse: and, at half an hour before midday, I drove into the yard of its ample premises.

END OF THE FIRST VOLUME.